Workbook 4/**Putting It All Together**

Phil Metzger

Cincinnati, Ohio

To Shirley Porter

Acknowledgments
When North Light asked me to consider writing a set of workbooks on perspective, my greedy eyes lit up and I said, "SURE!" I figured perspective was a snap and I could knock it off in a few weeks. Now, months older and somewhat chastened, I realize that there's more to the subject than meets the eye. There are thick books about perspective that dig deep into the mathematics and mystery of the subject. My job was to come up with skinny books that dispelled the mystery and concentrated on those aspects of perspective that someone in the "fine arts" would need to know. If you're an architect or an engineer, these workbooks are not for you. But if you draw and paint as a hobby or for a living, I think you'll find them just about right.

I want to thank two people who participated in producing these workbooks: Linda Sanders, my excellent editor at North Light, who kept steering me in the direction a workbook must take and really worked with me rather than sit back and accept whatever I threw her way; and Shirley Porter, who supplied a couple of the sketches in the workbooks, but who mainly read my prose before I submitted it to Linda and savagely deleted most (but not all) of the dumber things I had written. I honestly thank you both.

Perspective: the science of painting and drawing so that objects represented have apparent depth and distance. . . .
The Merriam-Webster Dictionary

Perspective Without Pain: Putting It All Together. Published by North Light, an imprint of F&W Publications, 1507 Dana Avenue, Cincinnati, Ohio 45207.

Manufactured in Hong Kong. First edition.

93 92 91 90 89 88 5 4 3 2 1

ISBN 0-89134-272-9

Editor: Linda Sanders
Designer: Clare Finney

Introduction

The first three workbooks have covered all the basic perspective techniques you might need in the fine arts. As you have seen, the technique called linear perspective heads the list, but the other techniques—overlap, size and space variation, modeling, detail and edges, and color and value change—are also important and effective.

In this workbook we tidy up a few loose ends. Some of the topics here elaborate on techniques already discussed and show how to apply those techniques to more advanced problems. Other topics, such as shadows, reflections, and refraction, might be considered secondary perspective techniques—they sometimes affect the illusion of depth, sometimes not—and so they are briefly treated here. And finally, we offer reminders of common errors in perspective and some cautions about the limitations of the use of perspective techniques.

Materials

The things you'll need for this workbook are some pencils (2B-soft, HB-medium, and 2H-hard will suffice), or charcoal if you prefer; some tracing paper; a straightedge; a flat mirror a foot or more square; a flashlight; a spray bottle; cardboard; scissors; and a few other odds and ends.

Details, Details

Most of the time when we discuss the illusion of depth in our pictures, there is the implication that we mean quite measurable depth—miles, perhaps, or at least feet. But there is another way of looking at the notion of "depth." Instead of thinking always in terms of big distances, think about the solidity or three-dimensionality of a subject. If you can make a subject look three-dimensional, even if one of the dimensions is only an inch or two, you will have emphatically strengthened the illusion of depth on your flat picture surface. A significant way to achieve this feeling of solidity, this third dimension, is by including in your picture appropriate detail, as I'll demonstrate in the following examples.

Bricks

The **top** drawing shows some bricks in linear perspective. Notice that they are drawn according to the basic rules of linear perspective you've already learned: Right-slanting lines meet at a vanishing point to the right, left-slanting lines meet at the left, and short vertical lines remain vertical.

Suppose we embellish the bare sketch with some detail. Draw along with me right on the first sketch. First let's get rid of the ruler-perfect edges. Real bricks just aren't so neat. They usually have imperfect edges, cracks, and chips.

Next we need to show thicknesses. Bricks are laid in mortar in a variety of ways. One of the most common is with the mortar slightly recessed.

Now let's add some texture and settle on a light source, **bottom**. I've chosen a source at the upper right, so the shadows I get are cast to the left and underneath each brick. The entire left wall, where the bricks turn a corner, is in shadow.

By the way, when you're establishing the values (lightness or darkness) of two adjacent areas like this bricked corner, it's usually helpful to make the dark side darkest near the corner. This emphasizes the value contrast that happens at the corner, and helps create a stronger illusion of a break, which in turn enhances the feeling of depth. This extra darkening where the two edges meet is not just a ploy to get more depth—it's actually how we see such a situation. The dark edge next to the light edge seems darker than it is because of the contrast with the light edge.

Details

You can see that including a little detail can inject life into some dull objects. You don't need to be working close to the subject, however, to get results. Suppose you're drawing a brick wall from a distance and you're confronting it squarely, not at an angle. Your basic bricks may look like the drawing at **right**.

Not too exciting. Let's see if a little detail might perk them up.

I've done several things here to introduce some interest in this wall. What's important as far as perspective is concerned is that the simple addition of details such as the cast shadows under and alongside some of the bricks signals their thickness and helps transform the wall from flat and two-dimensional to solid and three-dimensional. Notice that I chose not to fill in the entire wall with detail. I included only enough to establish solidity and left the rest to the viewer's imagination. Leaving elements of your picture for the viewer to "fill in" unconsciously is one way to get his or her attention.

Siding

Another type of detail that can enhance the feeling of depth is the wood siding found on many of the buildings people like to paint. As in the case of brickwork, you can add interest to the building by noting the type of siding it has and becoming familiar enough with its details to include just enough to get that feeling of solidity we're after.

Here's one type of simple, beveled siding and some uncomplicated cast shadows, **right**.

Details

I keep coming back to shadows because they are one kind of detail that can be counted on to give some thickness, or depth, to a picture. If the siding is old and weathered, as in my previous sketch, you have some extra opportunity to include details such as nails, cracks, and peeling paint. From a little distance such siding might look like this if you're a neatnik.

But if you loosen up a little and either observe or invent some details, you'll get a drawing like this, **center**.

As in the case of the bricks, the added detail in the siding helps transform it from something flat and two-dimensional to an object having thickness, or depth. One type of detail that's helpful is the shadow cast by one piece of siding on another. That little strip of shadow tells the viewer that there is one object sticking out beyond the other—and that, in turn, means that there is some thickness, or depth, there.

Notice that even a sunken nailhead has a bit of shadow cast on it by the edge of the board into which it has sunk. The dark cracks and joints between some of the boards are details that help us out by suggesting recesses between the boards. If the boards had no thickness there would be no recesses. And the way the shadow of the tree jumps from one board to the next subtly tells us that those can't be flat boards—there must be thickness, a little ledge, between the bottom of one board and the top of the next. These are all small details, but together they destroy flatness and suggest depth.

There are many kinds of siding. It's up to you to take a close look, learn the personality of the siding you're drawing, and include its essence in your picture. If you want to draw a building convincingly you'll need to pay attention to its clothes just as you would a model's clothes. At **bottom** are some more examples of sidings you may find.

Details

Roofs

The details you observe in buildings vary enormously from one part of the country to another. I'm most familiar with buildings in the East. If you happen to be from Florida or the Southwest you may see lots of stucco and little in the way of wood siding. Wherever you are, you have to get your nose right up close to your subjects and get to know them. As I write this I happen to be in a California motel waiting to give away a daughter in marriage tomorrow. Just out the window I see tile roofs, **top right**, unlike those I see in the East.

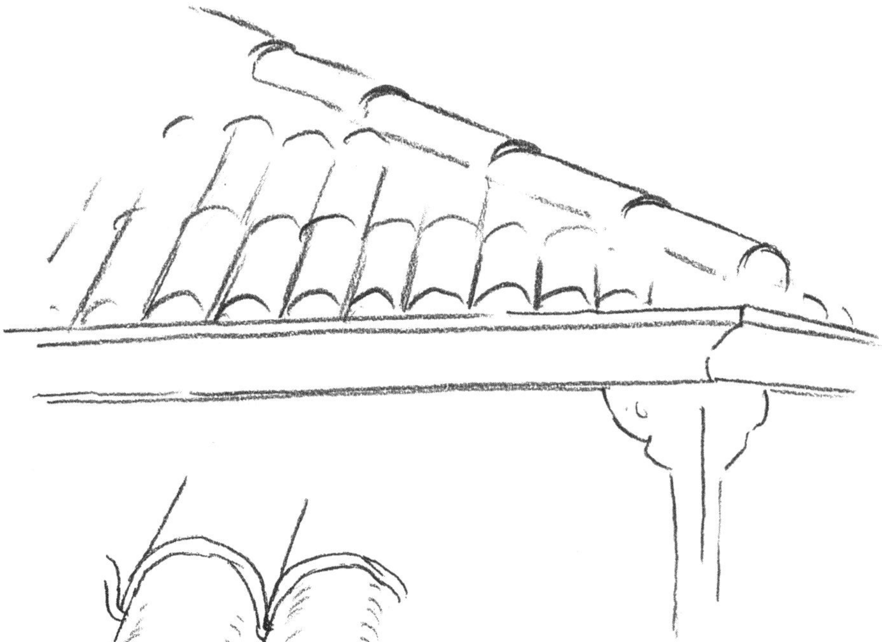

A closer look shows me how the tiles are overlapped to lead water down and off the roof instead of through it. They look something like the close-up at **center right**.

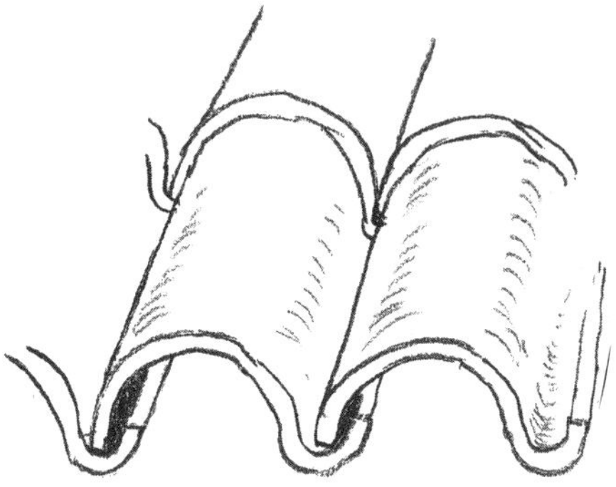

This overlapping is similar to the way asphalt or cedar or slate shingles shown in the two drawings **below right** and **far right**. Notice that the rows of tiles are roughly cylindrical and they go off into the distance the way any cylinder would—that is, the roughly circular ends appear elliptical, and the parallel rows of tiles converge toward a vanishing point.

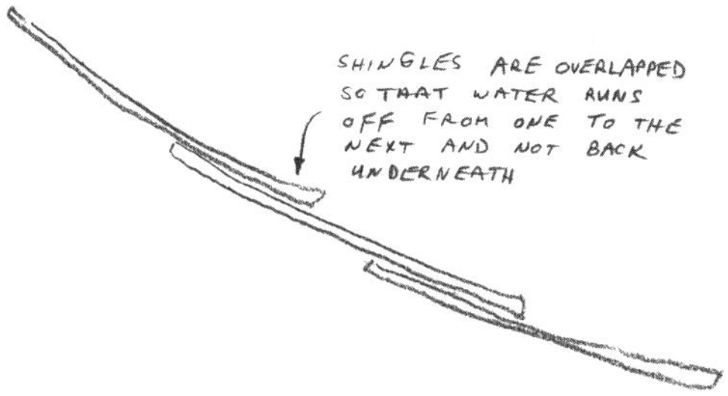

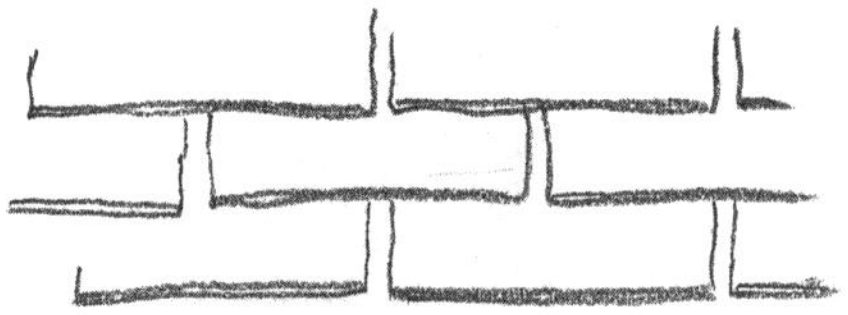

The point of this discussion is not to make you a housebuilder. I'm only trying to emphasize that whatever subject you draw, you need to observe its details if you expect to draw it with authority. If I had no idea how tiles were laid, for instance, I might draw them like the sketch at **bottom right** and end up with the world's leakiest roof. Anyone who knew better would glance at my drawing or painting, snort, and go on to someone else's work, convinced that I didn't know what I was doing.

You don't need to include tons of detail in your picture—in fact, that's often a mistake. What you should pursue is just the right amount of detail (1) to establish perspective and (2) to make your picture work overall. What the "right amount" is, of course, can't be determined by formula. It's a matter of artistic intuition, and what works for one artist will not be right for another. The amount of detail you include will change throughout your artistic life as your style and your taste and your subjects change. One thing is certain, however—the more you understand about the detail of your subject, the more confident you'll become about what to leave out. In a Dale Carnegie course on making speeches, the student is told to know forty times as much about his subject as he intends to include in a given speech. Having all that understanding stored away gives him the confidence to choose wisely the few nuggets he'll present to his audience.

Let's return for a moment to the subject of these workbooks. Perspective: techniques for attaining an illusion of depth. The use of detail is one of those techniques, but it in turn utilizes some of the others, such as overlap, modeling, size variation, and linear perspective. Effective use of perspective nearly always involves a marriage of a number of techniques, rather than a solo performance.

Exercise 1/**Details**

In each pair of sketches, "finish" the light one in a manner similar to mine to get a feel for the impact of detail on perspective. Don't be put off by the fact that you're "only" copying—the idea is to see how detail can nudge a flat sketch away from its flatness and give it a sense of depth. In each case, be sure to select a light source position before you start. Your light source need not be the same as mine. If mine is on the right, you might place yours on the left.

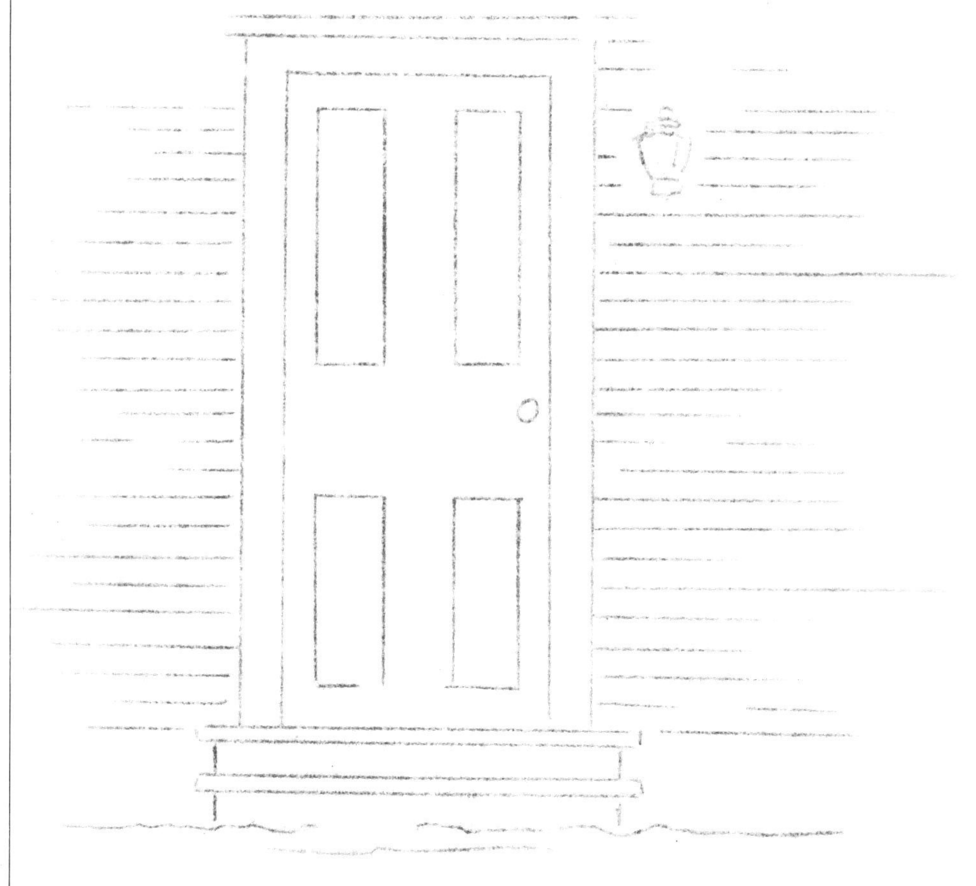

Exercise 1/**Details**

Exercise 1/**Details**

Sketch by Shirley Porter.

More Carpentry

So far in these workbooks we've drawn lots of boxy houses and barns, but we haven't added many of the features that give these buildings their unique personalities; we've kept them simple in order not to obscure their basic lines. The differences among buildings are endless and we can't hope to cover them all, but we can study a few examples that will serve as a foundation for drawing building details you're likely to encounter. What we'll be concerned with here are parts of buildings where linear perspective is important.

Dormers

First let's tackle a dormer. That's a structure stuck onto a sloping roof and containing a window. They come in lots of shapes and sizes, including the ones shown **below**.

What might get confusing is figuring out the funny angles where the dormer intersects the house's roof. Happily, you don't have to. Start with things you're familiar with—rectangular boxes whose lines recede to vanishing points—and the funny angles will take care of themselves.

More Carpentry

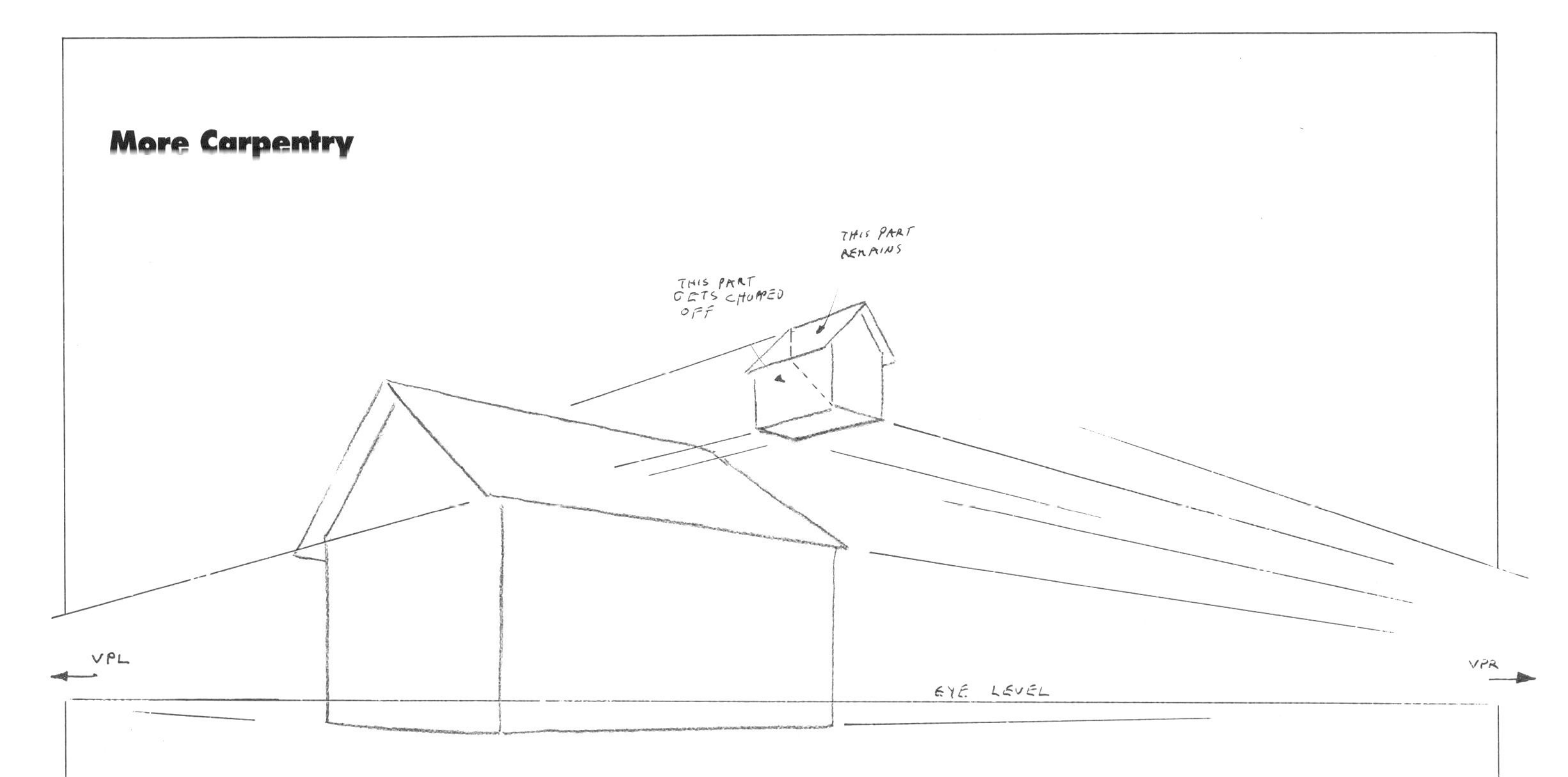

Think of a dormer as a little house set at right angles to a bigger house, **above**.

First you have to decide where to place the dormer on the roof. A single dormer will often be centered. If there are two or more, you'll have to decide just where the dormers are to be located in your drawing either by using your powers of artistic observation (that is, guessing) or by doing some more elaborate construction. If you're going to be fussy about all this, you'll find a section later on in this workbook that will help you with the matter of accuracy.

Next draw the major lines of the dormer. Remember that this little dormer, like a doghouse sticking out of the main roof, obeys all the "rules" of linear perspective. Its horizontal lines will recede to the same vanishing points as those of the main house. If this were a weird dormer set at an odd angle to the house, this would not be so, but that's a rarity.

As shown at **right**, the dormer's roofline (*b*) should slope toward the left and hit VPL, the same vanishing point hit by the left-slanting lines of the main house. The bottom edge of the dormer (*c*) will slant toward VPR.

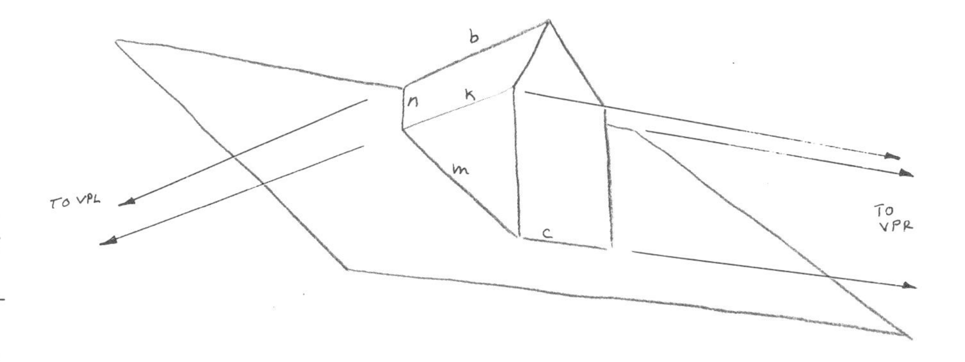

The steps for drawing the front shape of the dormer are the same as those we followed while drawing houses in Workbook 2. But how do we determine the lines showing the intersection of the dormer and the main roof? It's easy if you realize that the lower edge of the dormer's little roof, line *k*, goes to VPL and that line *m*, where the side of the dormer meets the main roof is parallel to the front edge of the main roof. Line *n* shows where the dormer's roof intersects the house's roof. Where this line falls depends on the view you choose from which to do your drawing. Draw the other lines first and let them dictate where this one ends up.

Exercise 2/**Dormers**

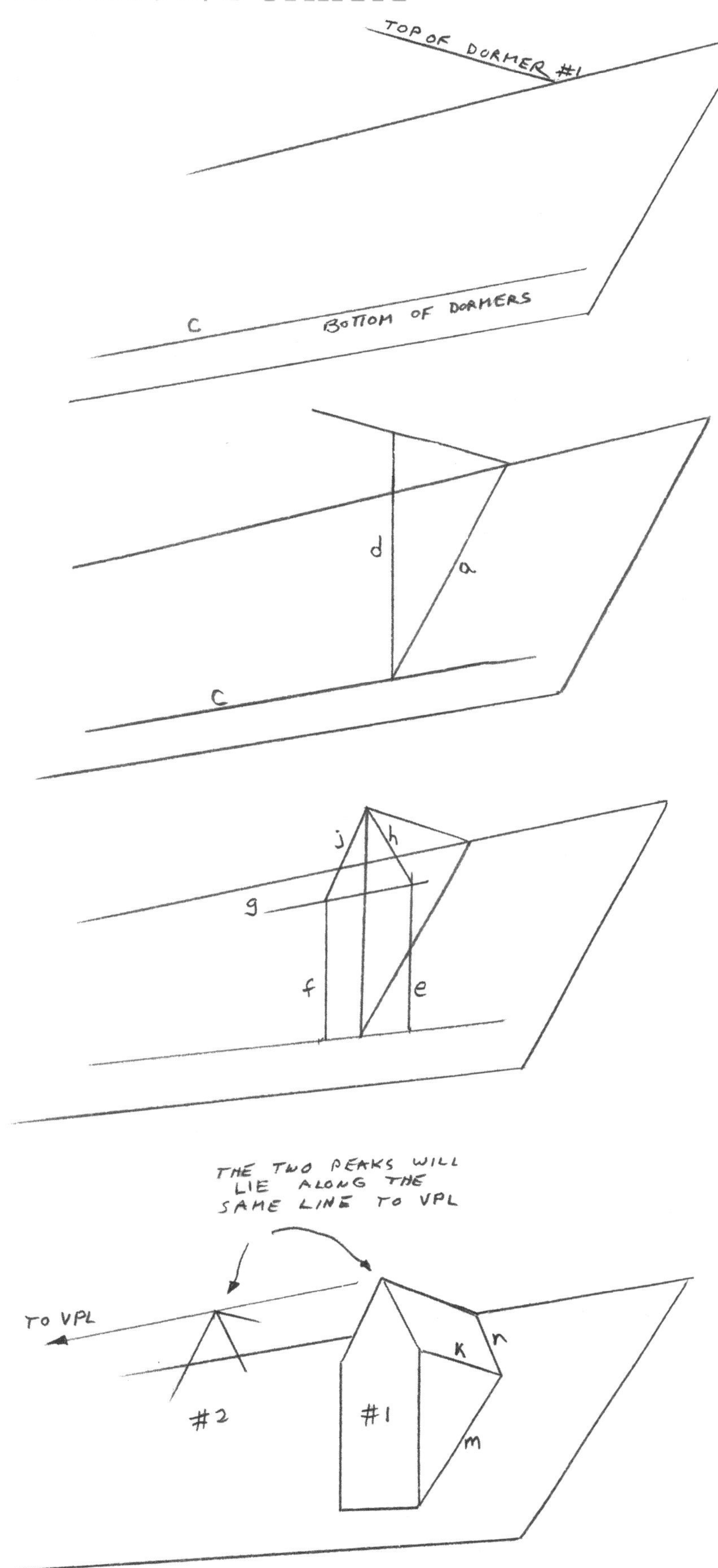

On page 11 is one side of a slanted roof. The problem is to build two dormers ("gabled" dormers, as illustrated in the text). I've shown where the peak of each dormer's roof is to meet the peak of the main roof of the house. I've also shown the slant of the top of the roof of the nearer dormer (#1). Do dormer #1 first, since the second dormer will be partly hidden by the near one. The steps would be as follows:

Step 1: Draw line *c* to indicate where the bottom edges of the dormers are to meet the roof.

Step 2: Draw line *a* parallel to the front edge of the roof. Draw vertical line *d* through the intersection of *a* and *c*. Line *d* divides the front face of the dormer in two (in perspective).

Step 3: Draw lines *e, f,* and *g,* defining the rectangular part of the face of the dormer. The heights of *e* and *f* are up to you. Line *g* goes to VPL. Draw *h* and *j* to get the triangular portion of the face of the dormer.

Step 4: Draw line *k* toward VPR; draw line *m* parallel to the front edge of the roof. Finally draw line *n*. Then add dormer roof overhang, window, and other details.

Draw dormer #2 the same way. Depending on the position from which these dormers are being viewed, and also on how wide you chose to make dormer #1 and how far out from the main roof you decided to build it, portions of dormer #2 may be hidden behind #1. Although dormer #2, because of perspective, will appear smaller than #1, their shapes will be the same (again, allowing for perspective distortions).

Exercise 2/**Dormers**

Directions for this exercise are on page 10.

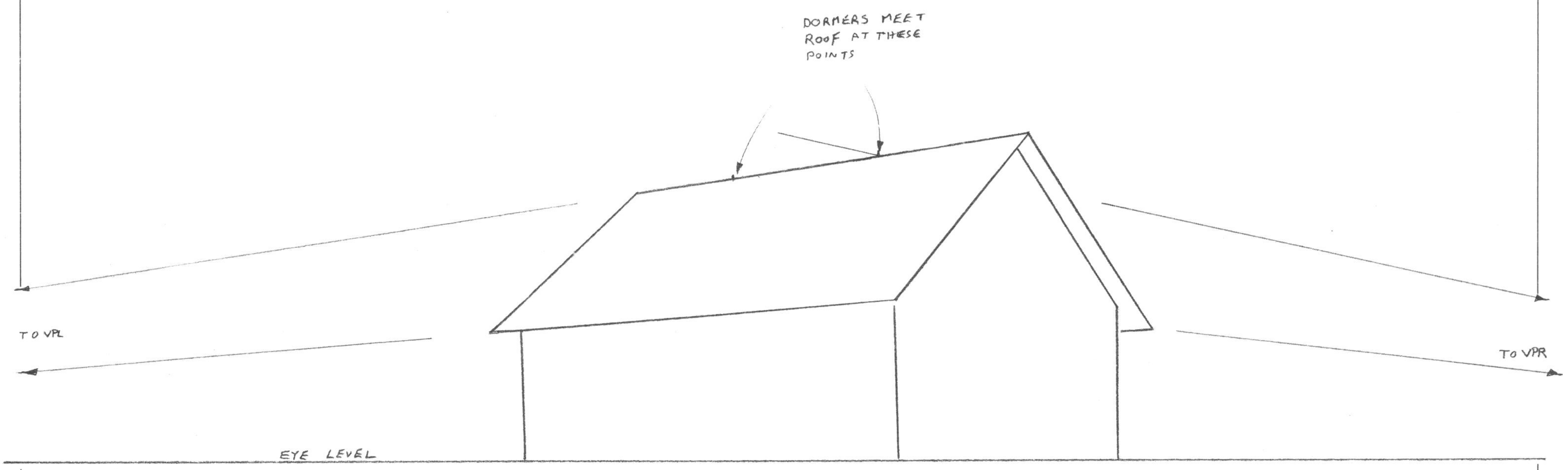

More Carpentry

Windows and Doors

Another bit of carpentry that often eludes an artist who doesn't look closely at the subject is the construction of windows and doors. If you're drawing from a great enough distance, it doesn't much matter, but in close-up views your understanding of these building details can be important.

For example, consider the difference between the two windows, **above**. The left-hand drawing shows some understanding of how a certain type of window is built. It's a so-called "double-hung" window; the upper and lower halves slide up and down independently. In the left-hand sketch, the lower window is shown recessed—that is, the upper window overlaps the lower. They're always that way, like shingles on a roof, so the rainwater will not get inside the house. The sketch at the right has little depth; it does nothing to convince us it's real.

There's something else to watch out for in drawing such things as windows. Although this has little to do with perspective, I think it rates a mention here. Avoid unreasonable placement of windows in a building, such as the goofs **below**.

In the first, we have a window looking out from a chimney. In the second, the upper two windows are too low. In the third example, the upper windows are too high. You can avoid discrepancies like the last two if you mentally place people in your building and see how they fit.

More Carpentry

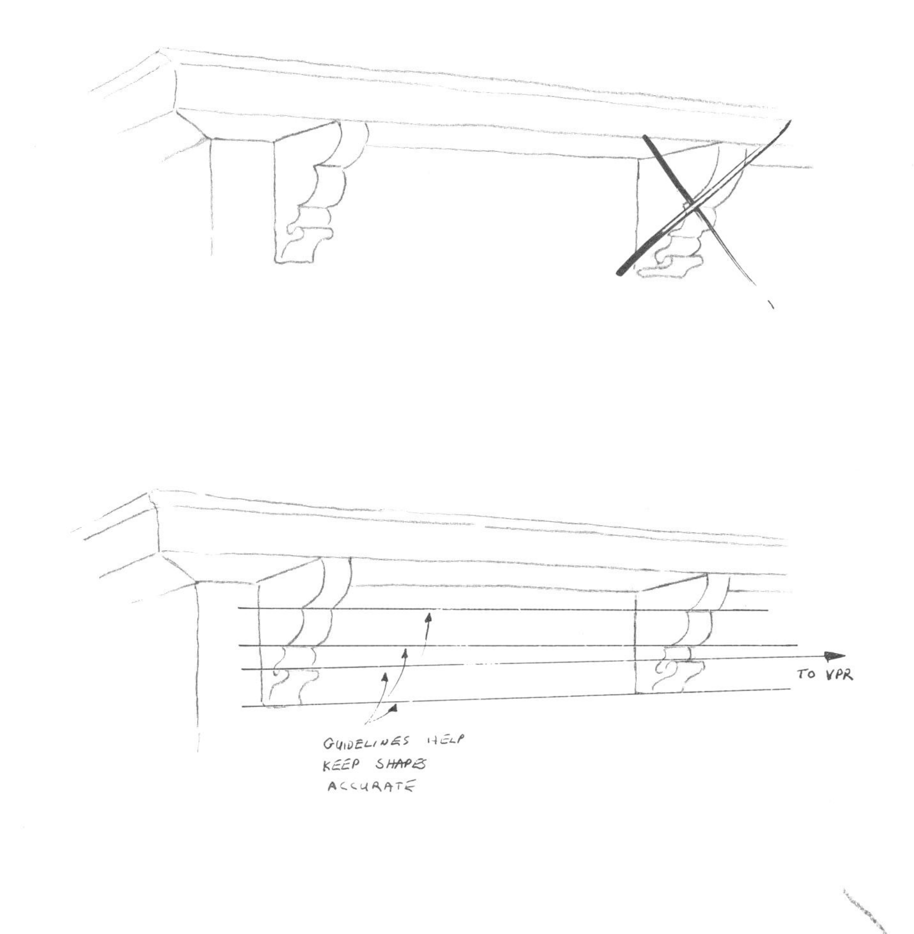

Trim

There are a trillion different kinds of trim you'll encounter on various buildings. You can use trim not only to decorate your painting but to enhance perspective as well. It's easy to be thrown off in your drawing when copying such shapes as those at **top left** and trying to get them all the same shape! You may forget to draw the bracket that's farther away smaller than the one closer to you, for example.

You'll find that if you first draw one of the decorative brackets to your satisfaction and then run some light perspective guidelines, drawing the remaining brackets will be much easier than trying to draw each bracket independent of the others, **center left**.

Another example of "trim" is what often appears at the edge of a barn or shed roof, where the roof rafters are simply allowed to show rather than be concealed under some nailed-on boards, **bottom**.

Such construction offers the artist a chance to include a bit of interesting detail. Although it's doubtful that barns were built this way for reasons other than economy, the same idea is carried forth in many houses today to provide a rustic look.

Exercise 3/**Brackets and Spindles**

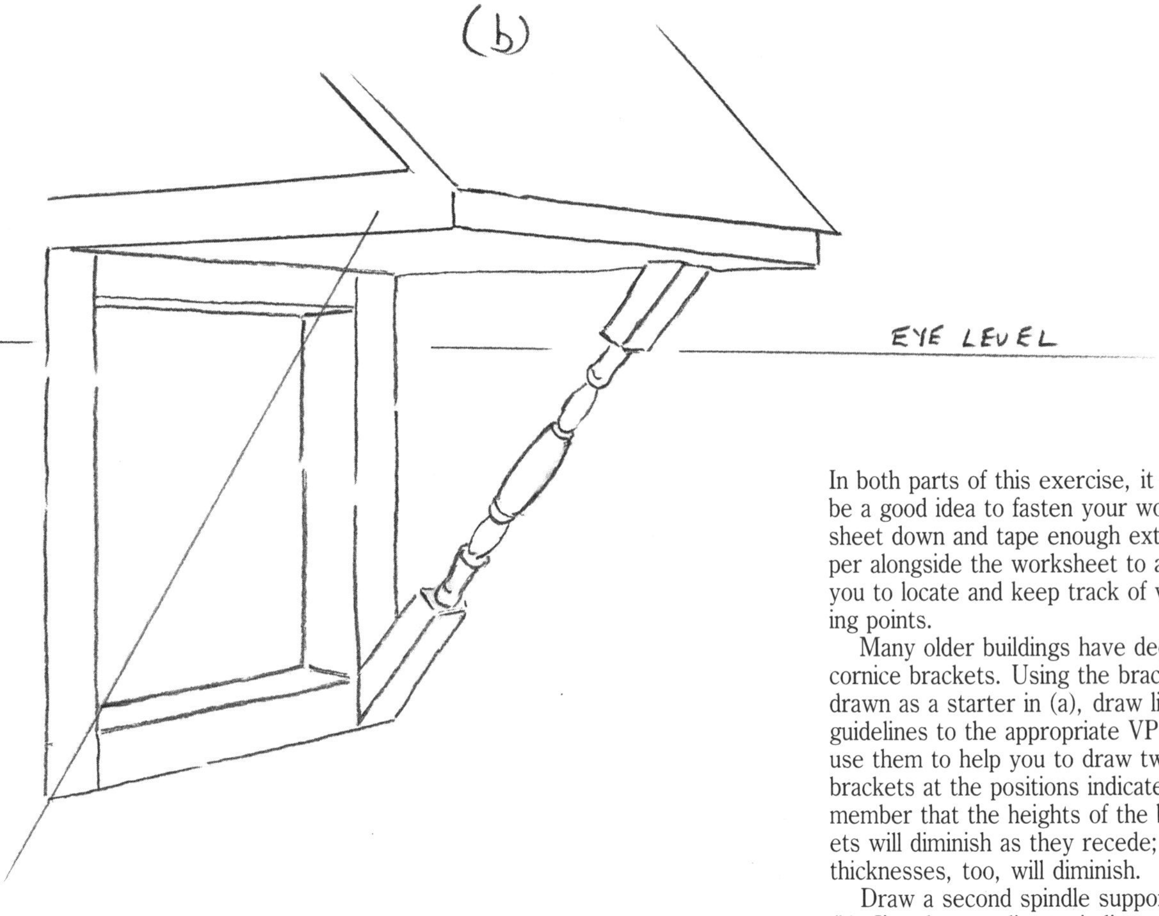

In both parts of this exercise, it would be a good idea to fasten your worksheet down and tape enough extra paper alongside the worksheet to allow you to locate and keep track of vanishing points.

Many older buildings have decorative cornice brackets. Using the bracket I've drawn as a starter in (a), draw light guidelines to the appropriate VP and use them to help you to draw two more brackets at the positions indicated. Remember that the heights of the brackets will diminish as they recede; their thicknesses, too, will diminish.

Draw a second spindle support in (b). I've drawn a line to indicate the location of the nearest edge of the spindle you are to draw.

Projection

Frequently artists need to place lines on a curved surface to represent evenly spaced spokes in a wheel, flutes or grooves in a column, windows in a rounded tower, and the like. I'll demonstrate an easy way to do this, using spokes, as detailed in the lesson beginning at right. This method is called projection.

Spokes

If a circular object such as a wheel is viewed straight on, with no perspective involved, it's easy enough to draw its spokes. The wheel can simply be divided and subdivided as many times as you wish to get the appropriate number of spokes, **right**.

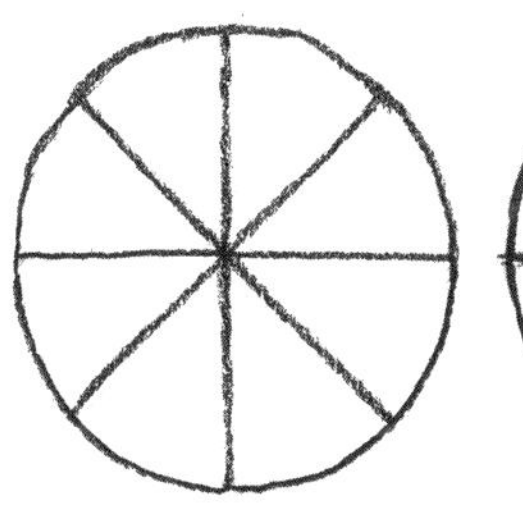

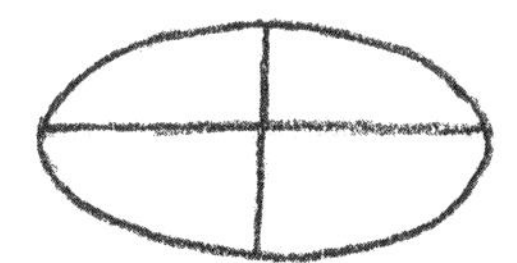

Suppose this wheel is thrown into perspective, and we no longer have a circle but an ellipse. We can quickly find four of the spokes by drawing the two axes of the ellipse, but the remaining spokes are not quite so obvious. All we know intuitively is that the farther we get toward the skinny ends of the ellipse, the closer together the spokes

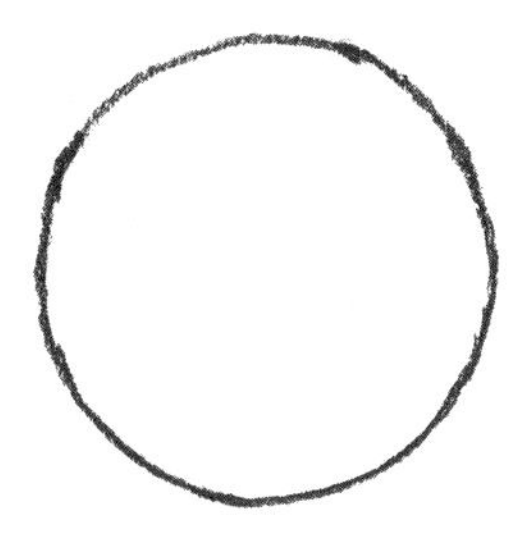

will appear. At the right is an approximate way of finding out how the spaces between the spokes vary. First, draw a circle above the ellipse with a diameter the same as the long dimension of the ellipse, **above.**

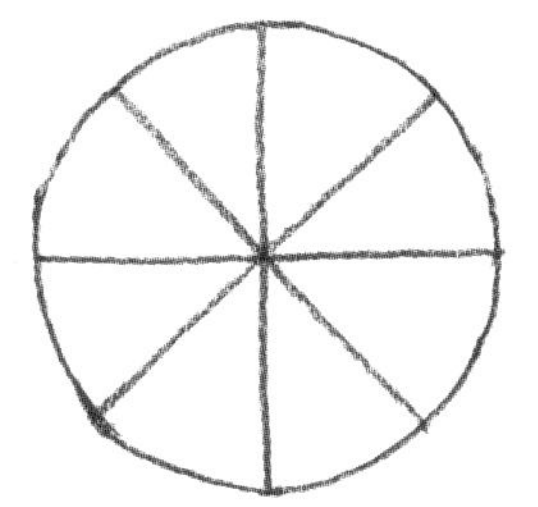

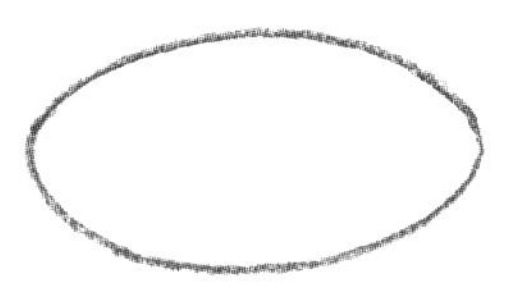

Next divide the circle, like a pie, into the number of equal slices you wish. Let's go with eight.

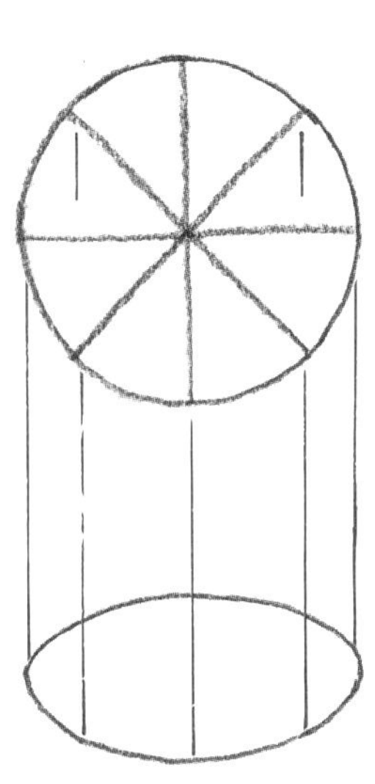

Then draw vertical lines down from where the spokes intersect the circle, to the ellipse.

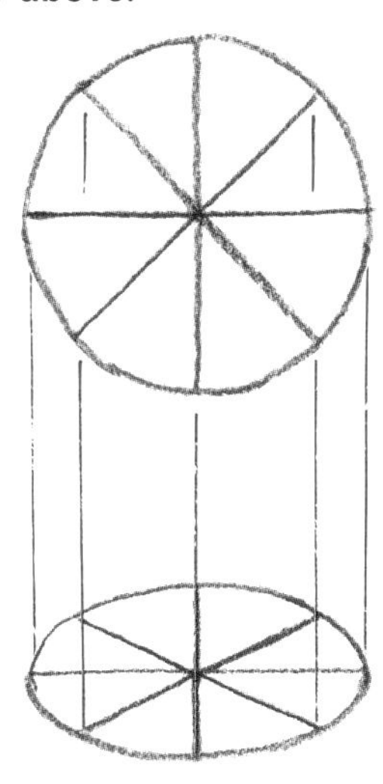

Now draw your spokes from the center of the ellipse to each point where the vertical lines hit the ellipse. The resulting wheel spokes are a reasonable approximation of what happens in perspective.

FOR MORE ACCURACY I MOVED THE "CENTER" BACK A LITTLE TO PLACE IT AT PERSPECTIVE CENTER

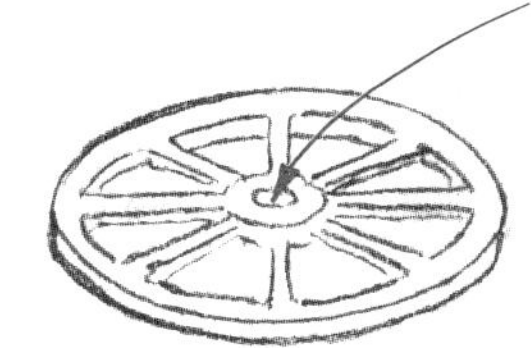

To get it more nearly right, move the center of the ellipse back a little to come closer to perspective center before you draw your spokes.

As you can see, projection means drawing guidelines from one view of an object to a second view of that object to determine where critical parts of the object will appear in the second view. We'll use projection further in the examples that follow.

Exercise 4/**Spokes**

Using the projection method, draw spokes in perspective in the ellipses corresponding to each circle. In the fourth example, show the width of each spoke in perspective.

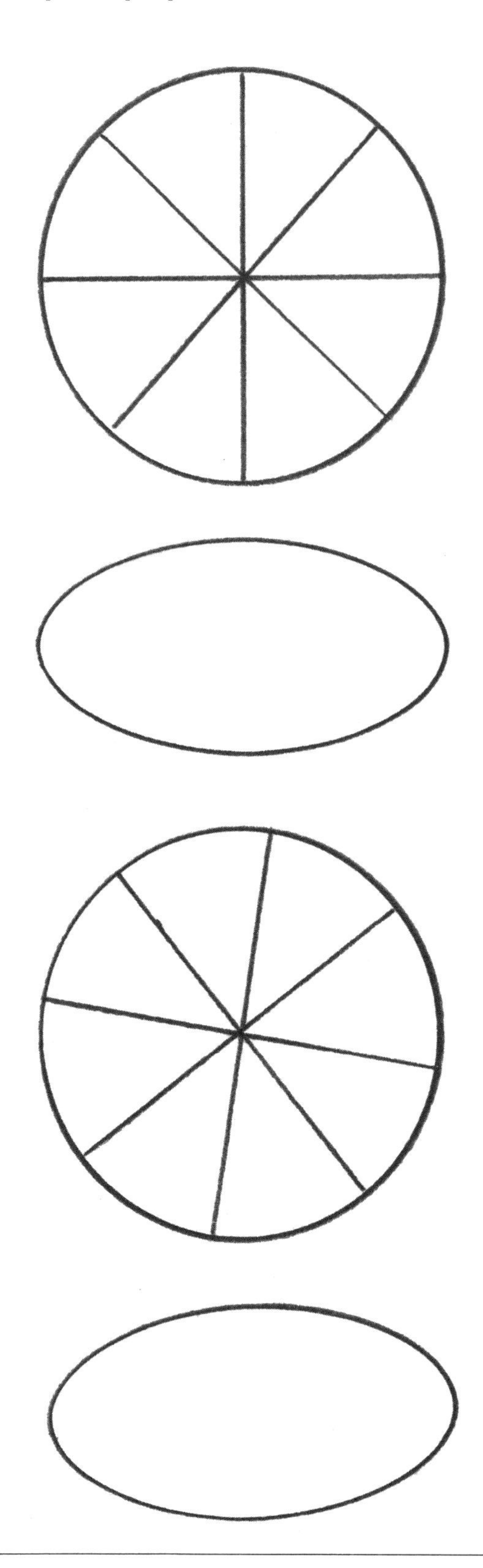

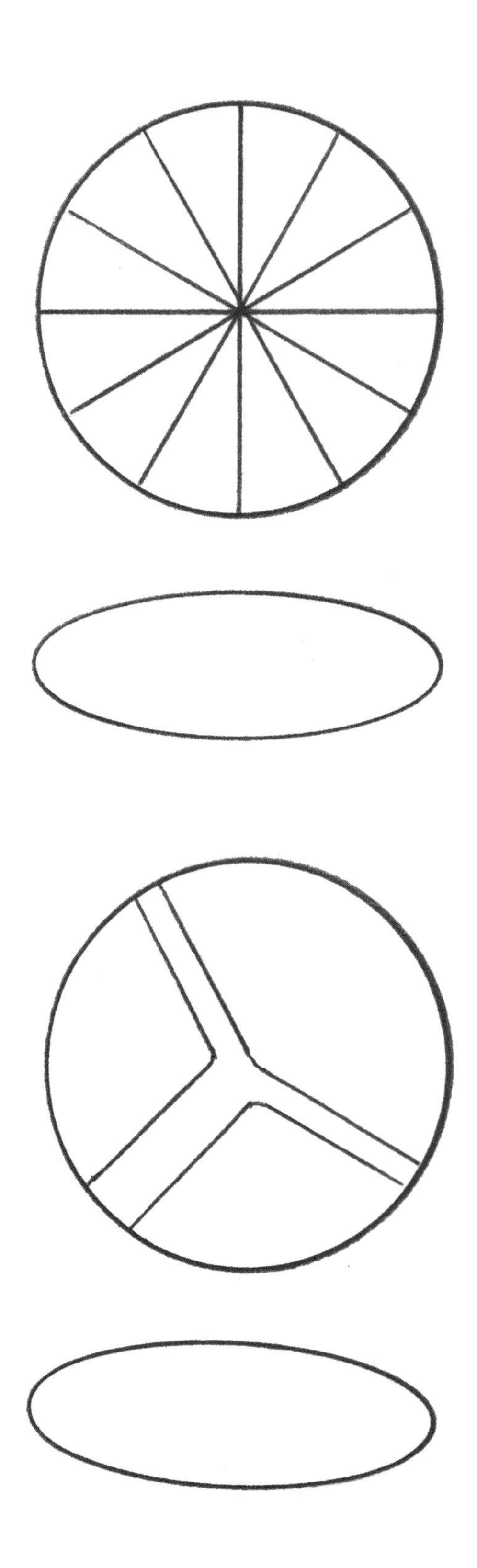

Projection

Flutes

We can extend our handling of spokes to other objects. Imagine you are drawing a fluted column. Let's say the end of the column looks something like this, with sixteen flutes, or grooves.

If we're viewing the column from its side, all that's necessary is to draw sixteen "spokes" in a circle above the column and draw vertical lines downward to show the placement of the flutes.

You can get as fancy as you want. If you'd like to project onto the column not only the locations of the flutes, but their widths, as well, then show the "spokes" in your circle as having appropriate thickness and project down twice as many vertical lines, **far right**.

Notice that the widths of the flutes gradually decrease in perspective as they get nearer the edges of the column. Notice, too, that you automatically get the proper widths of the ribs separating the flutes. In fact, the spokes in your circle can represent either the flutes or the ribs, whichever pleases you. One person's rib is another person's flute.

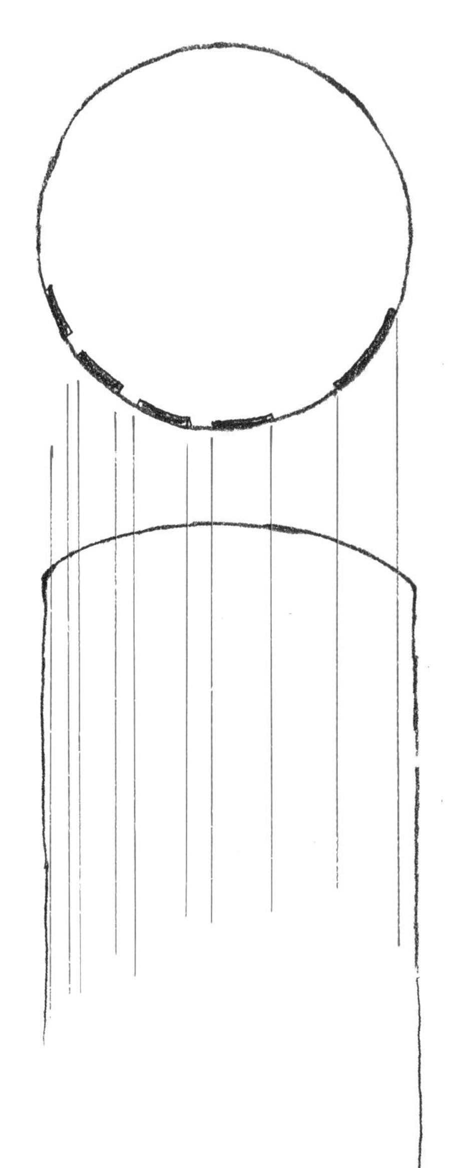

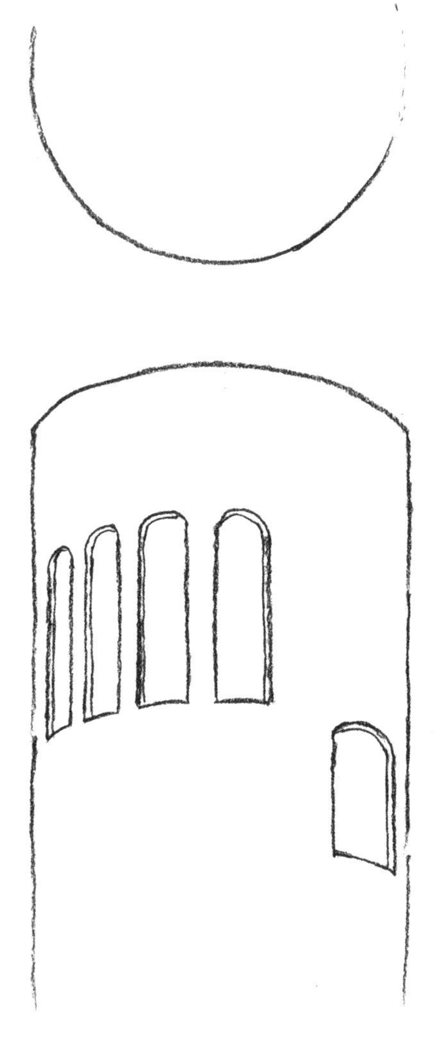

A Rounded Tower

The same sort of construction helps us to draw a rounded tower with windows. Start with an outline of your tower and a circle above it (or below it, whichever seems more comfortable), **left**. The diameter of the circle is the thickness of the tower.

Mark off pie slices on the circle to represent the widths of the windows. There's no need for the windows to be the same width as the spaces between them, of course. For that matter, the windows need not be the same size, nor evenly spaced, nor even on the same level. Let's say we have five windows, spaced and in the sizes shown at **center**. Drop vertical construction lines.

Now draw in the windows at an appropriate height. If we assume they are arched windows with flat sills, then in perspective they might look something like the drawing at **right**.

Exercise 5/**A Dome**

In this sketch you have a building's dome and a circular base. Between the dome and the base are to be thirteen columns. Using the projection method, place the thirteen columns. Start as usual by dividing a circle into thirteen equal slices and projecting down to the ellipses. You can get the thickness of the columns either by starting with thick spokes in your circle (the more accurate way), or add the appropriate thicknesses after you've placed the columns.

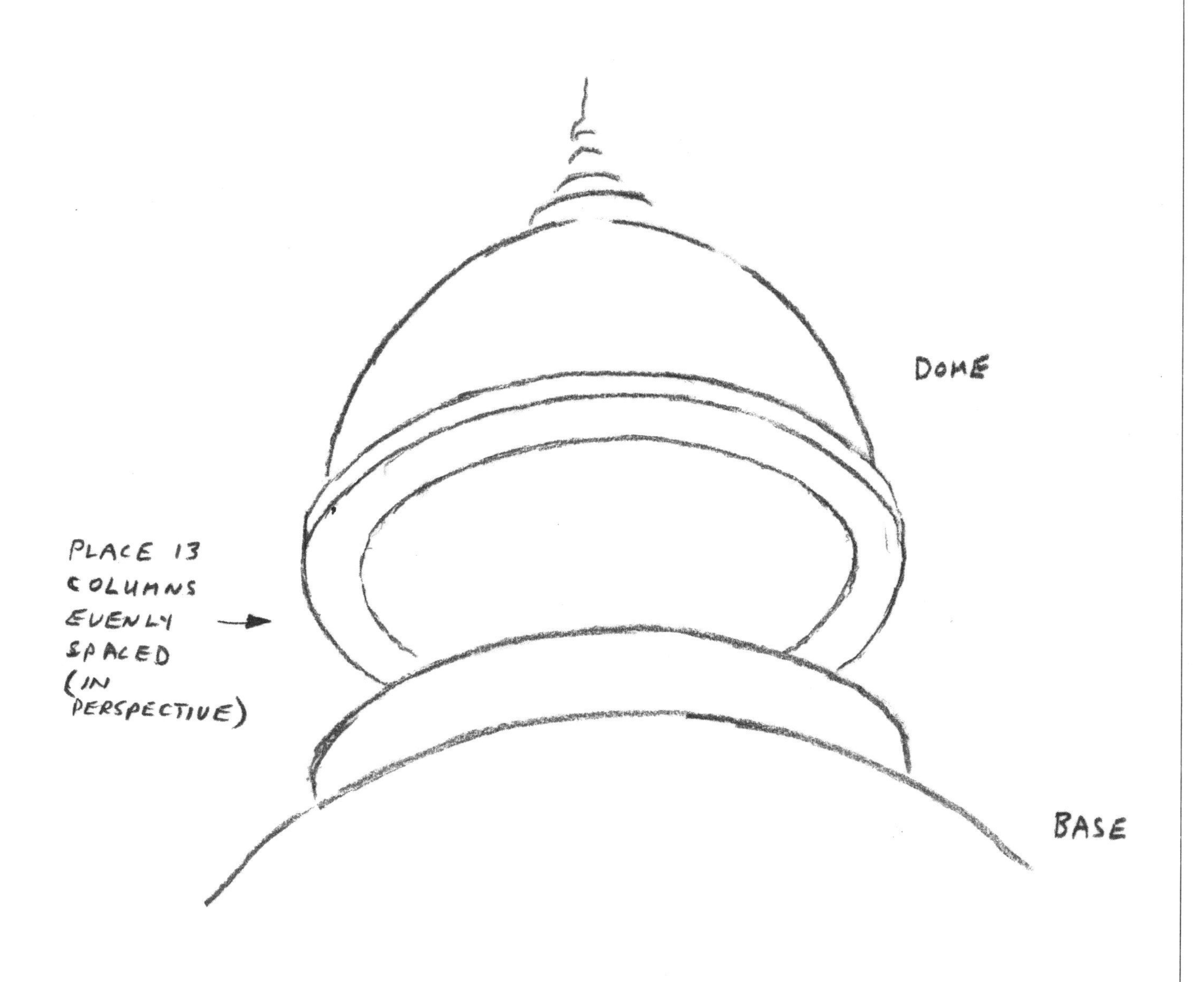

Some Extrapolations

The kind of construction we discussed in the last section will help you out in drawing lots of rounded subjects, including such grand things as monuments or capitol domes. But some subjects are not rounded and yet seem to pose similar drawing problems. Beginning at the right, we'll look at how simple it can be to draw more complex shapes.

Nuts!
Let's think small for a moment. How about drawing something like a nut or a bolt? You can probably find a loose nut around the house. It might look a little complicated to draw, but we can draw it using the spokes method. The nut I'm using as a model is hexagonal.

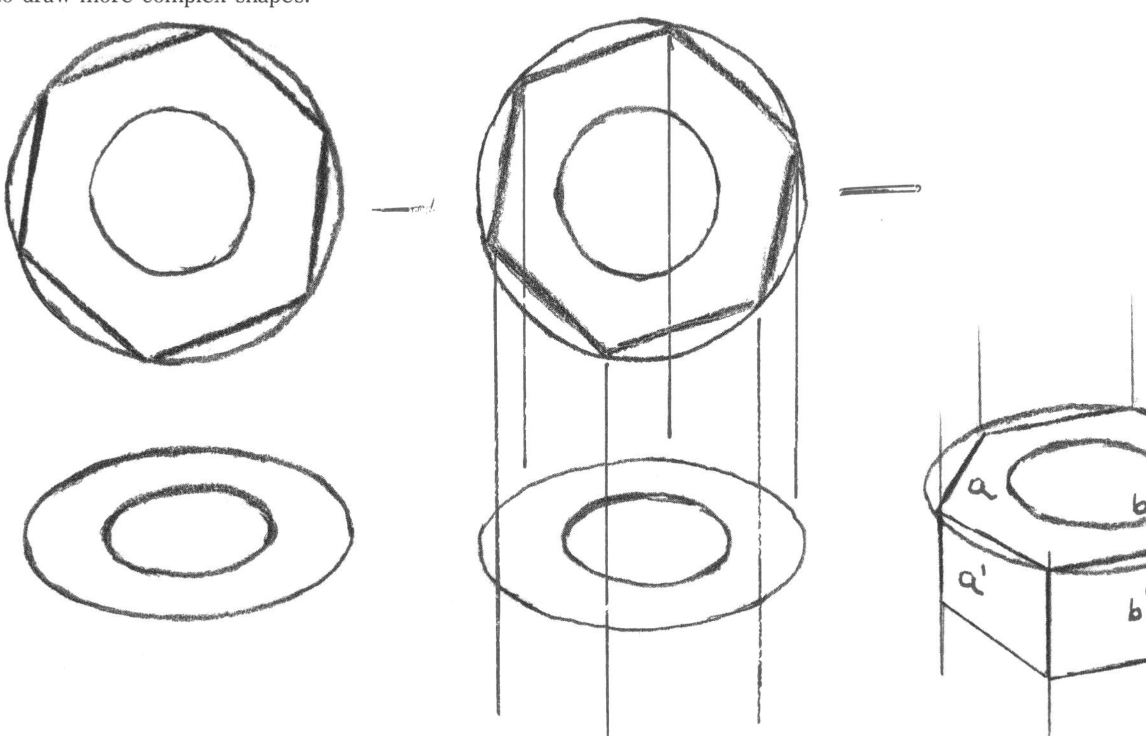

First, draw a circle whose diameter represents the nut at its widest dimension and draw the nut inside the circle in whatever position you choose. Then draw an ellipse under the circle. Make the ellipse as fat or as flat as you wish to get the amount of perspective you wish. Draw a smaller ellipse with the same perspective center, for the hole in the nut.

Drop vertical construction lines. Where they hit the ellipse, they define the points or edges of the nut.

Now connect the points and then extend the vertical edges of the nut downward as far as you judge necessary to show the nut's thickness. Lightly draw line a' parallel to a; b' parallel to b; and c' parallel to c. That'll be almost right, but not quite. Remember that we're seeing this object in perspective, so pairs of lines, such as a' and a, that we know are parallel in the actual object are not parallel when the object is seen in perspective. Those pairs of lines will all converge to vanishing points. All three vanishing points will be on your eye level. As in so many cases, you don't need to draw the converging lines, but simply slant a', b', and c' slightly more sharply upward than their counterparts, a, b, and c.

Finally, go ahead and have fun putting the finishing touches on your drawing.

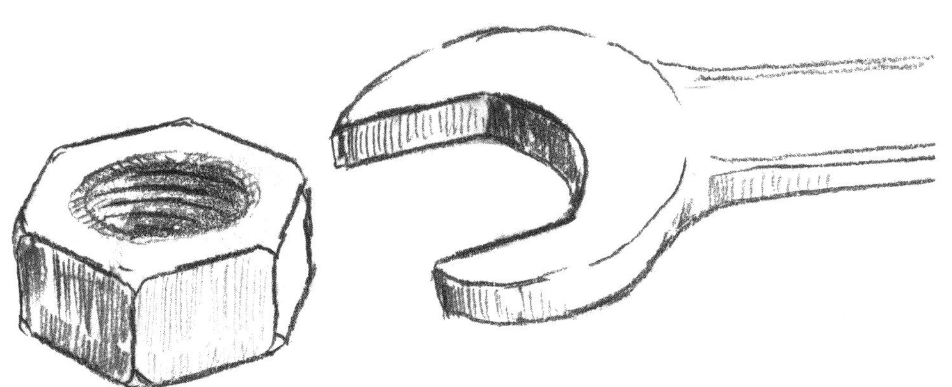

Some Extrapolations

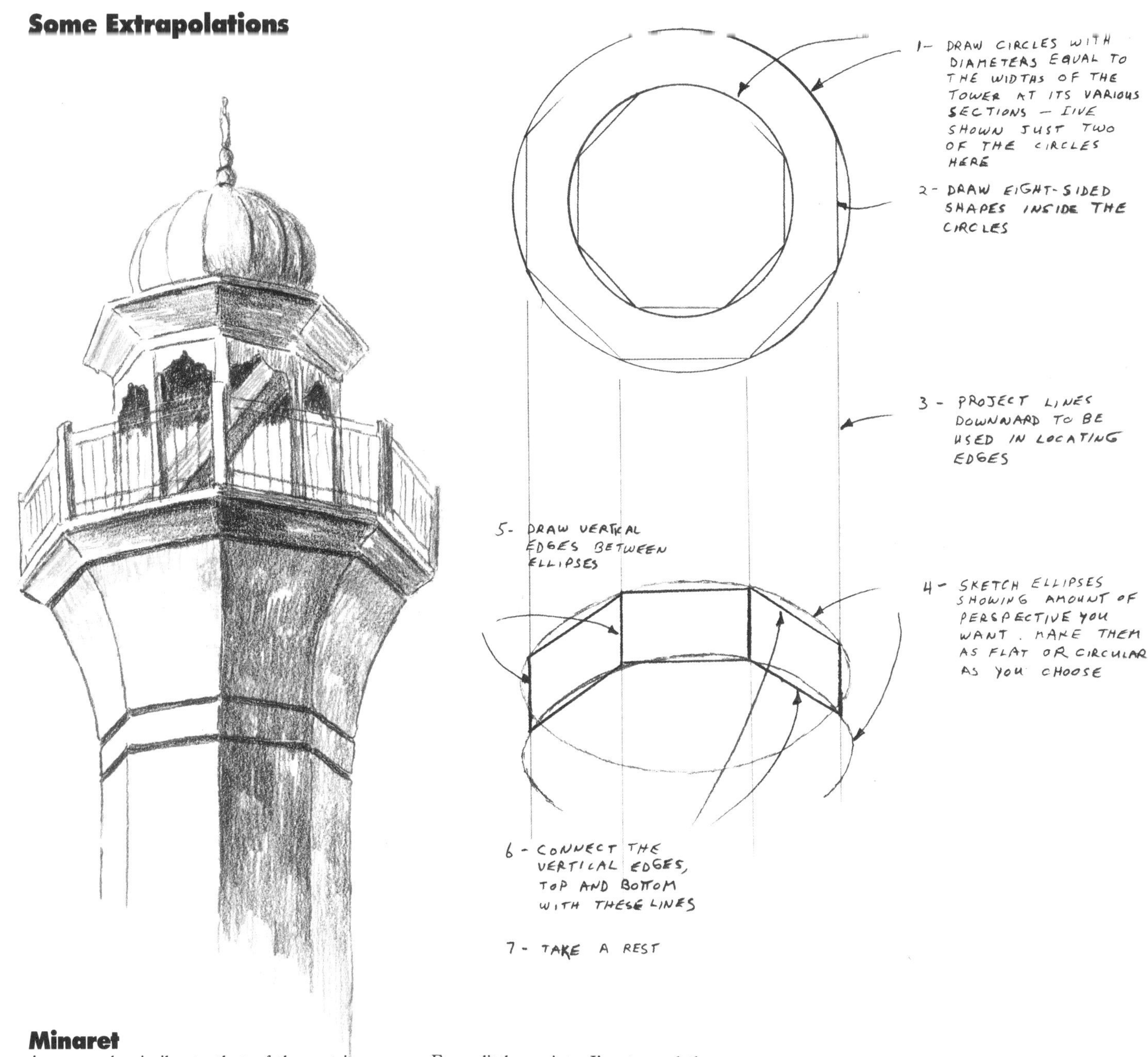

Minaret

An example similar to that of the nut is this minaret, **above**. The basic structure is octagonal. No matter how many sides an object has, if its cross-section can be fit into a circle, the spokes and flutes projection method will help you to draw it. The annotated drawings that follow will describe the drawing process. It may look complicated at first, but if you'll follow it step by step, you'll see that even complicated structures can be almost as easy as the nut we just drew.

For a little variety I've turned the structure at a different angle in the construction drawings. Whatever you do, don't get too wrapped up in the construction. Some of the steps that I show in this and other examples are only there to get your mental juices flowing in the right direction. Usually you can get by with just enough "construction" to place critical edges and then trust your drawing instincts from there.

Some Extrapolations

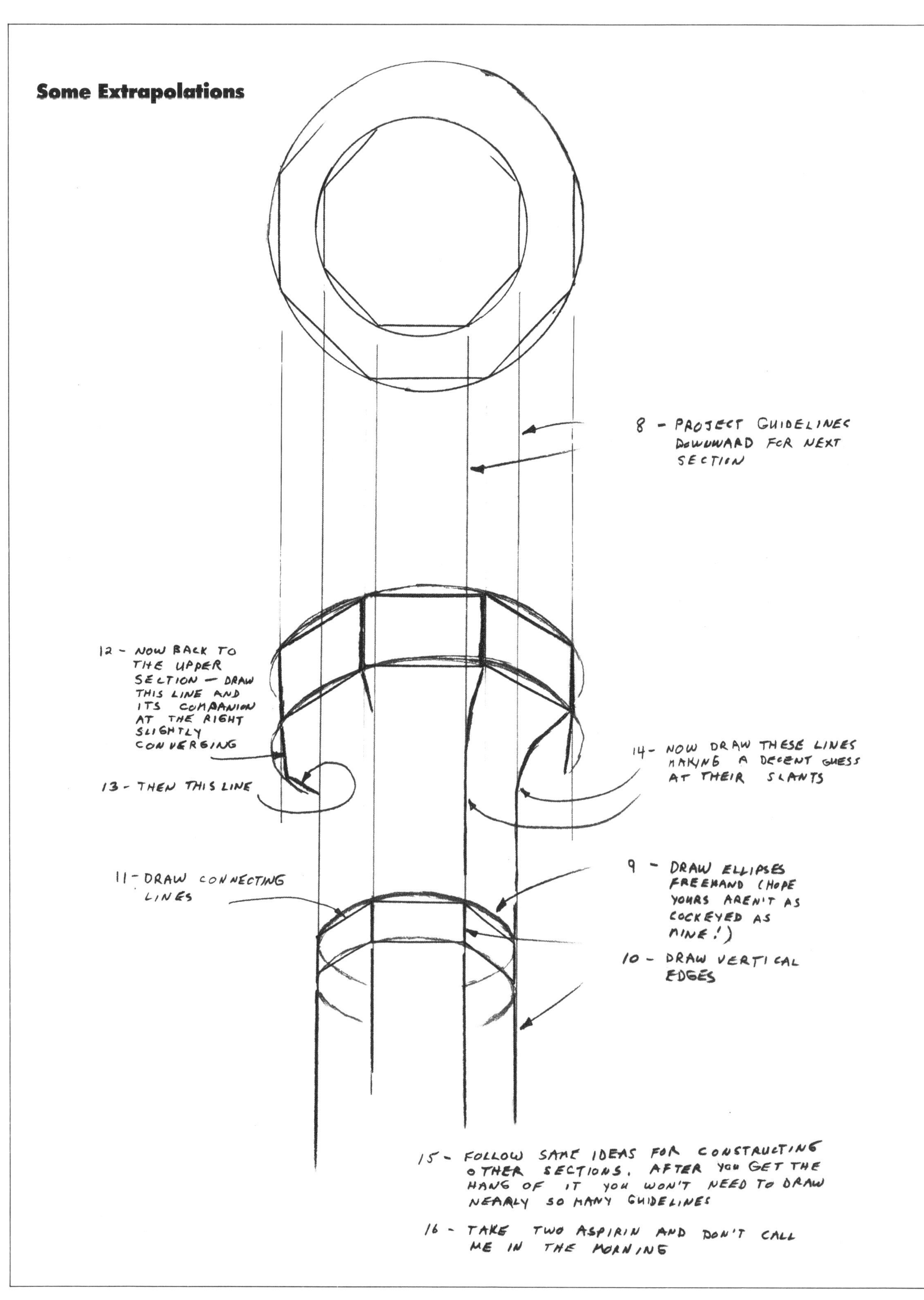

Beyond Eyeballing

Sometimes we get involved in subjects that demand more accuracy than is possible with casual eyeballing or thumb-and-pencil measurement. Here is a method of determining how evenly spaced objects of equal size diminish in size and spacing as they recede.

Upright Objects

Suppose you're drawing a neat row of utility poles stretching across a flat piece of land. The poles are all the same size and the spaces between them are all equal. How do you proceed?

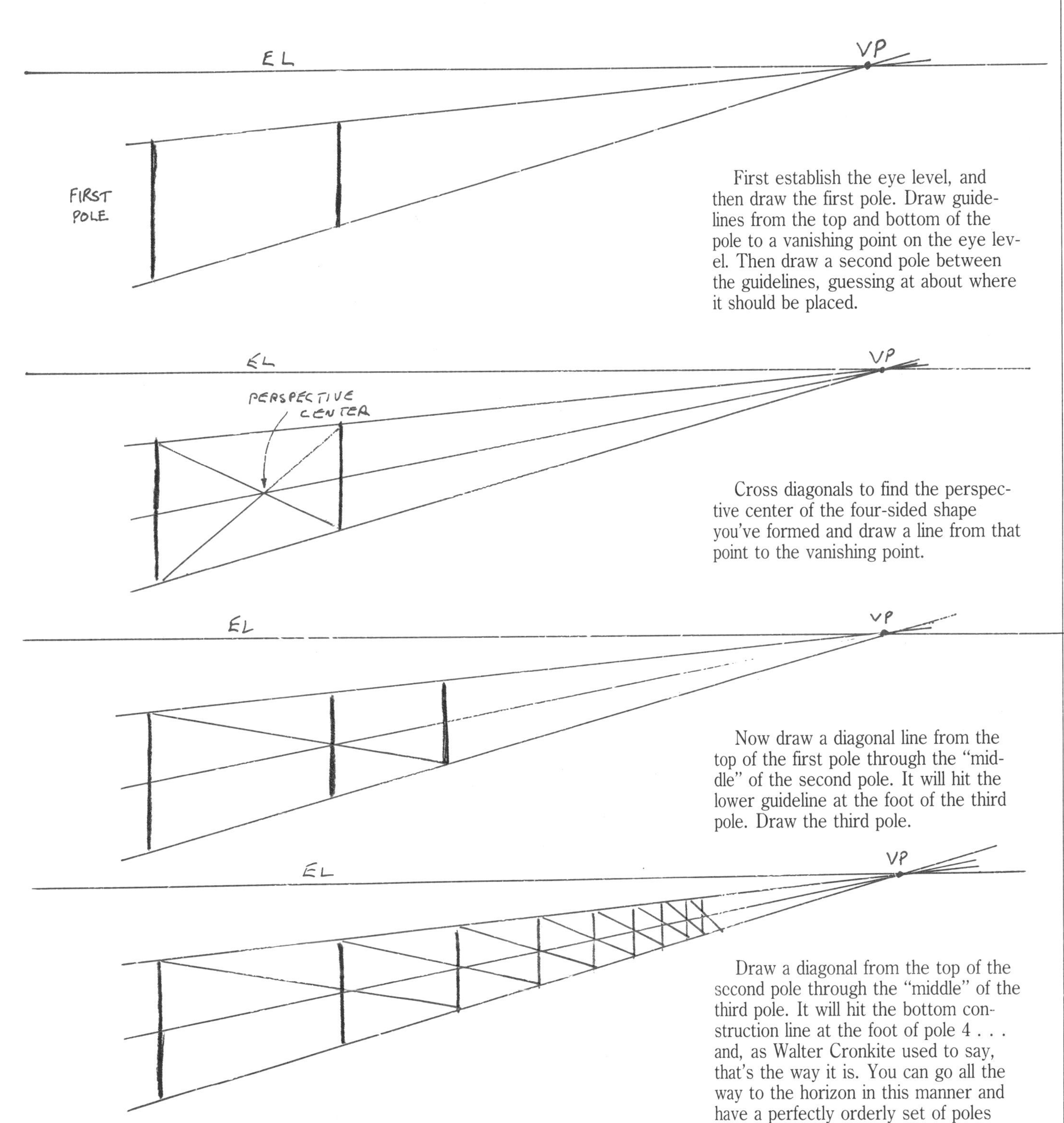

First establish the eye level, and then draw the first pole. Draw guidelines from the top and bottom of the pole to a vanishing point on the eye level. Then draw a second pole between the guidelines, guessing at about where it should be placed.

Cross diagonals to find the perspective center of the four-sided shape you've formed and draw a line from that point to the vanishing point.

Now draw a diagonal line from the top of the first pole through the "middle" of the second pole. It will hit the lower guideline at the foot of the third pole. Draw the third pole.

Draw a diagonal from the top of the second pole through the "middle" of the third pole. It will hit the bottom construction line at the foot of pole 4 . . . and, as Walter Cronkite used to say, that's the way it is. You can go all the way to the horizon in this manner and have a perfectly orderly set of poles when you're done.

Beyond Eyeballing

A Tile Floor

Perhaps more useful would be an example such as a tile floor. Sometimes we include them in interior paintings or still lifes, and if they're not right they'll ruin the painting by making the floor seem to tilt too much or not enough.

Suppose you're drawing a tile floor from a vantage point something like this. You've chosen your viewing position a little right of center (but it could have been at center or left of center).

We'll first draw this floor in one-point linear perspective. The vanishing point will be directly ahead of you—on the eye level, of course.

The reason for choosing one-point is this: when you are so close to a subject (you're standing right on the tile floor, let's say), a second vanishing point would be so far to your right or left that the lines converging toward that VP would have negligible slant. In other words, one-point perspective may be considered two-point perspective with one of the vanishing points out around Mars. For practical purposes, the lines in the tiles running right to left across the scene are parallel to the picture plane. If the floor were large enough—that is, if it stretched far enough away from the viewer—in that case there might be some discernible two-point perspective. An example a little later will illustrate this.

As you can see in the sketch **right**, I've drawn in the lines representing the rows of tiles (they could be floorboards at this point). How do you make them fan out properly? The easiest way, and accurate enough, is to mark off equal widths along the edge where the floor meets the far wall. Then draw lines through those points and the VP.

Next, pick a pair of horizontal lines near to you and sketch them in to define your first tile. These are like the first two poles in the earlier example; once you establish them, everything else becomes pretty mechanical. You may need to experiment a little to get these lines feeling right.

Draw right on this sketch and follow along with me through the rest of the steps.

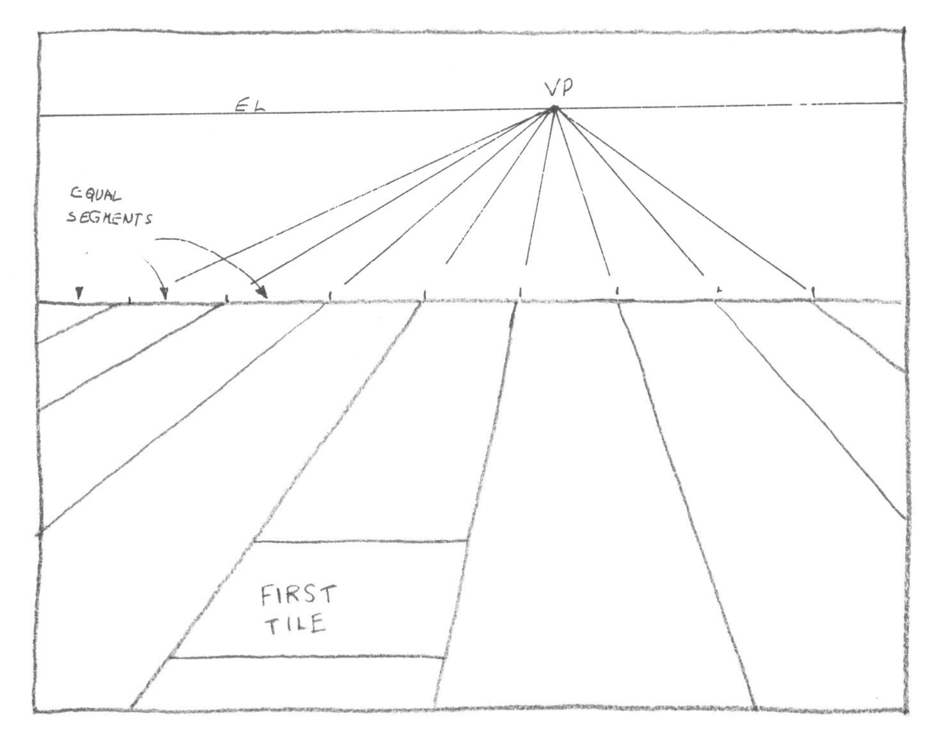

Beyond Eyeballing

Locate the perspective midpoint of the tile by crossing its diagonals, and draw a construction line through it to the VP.

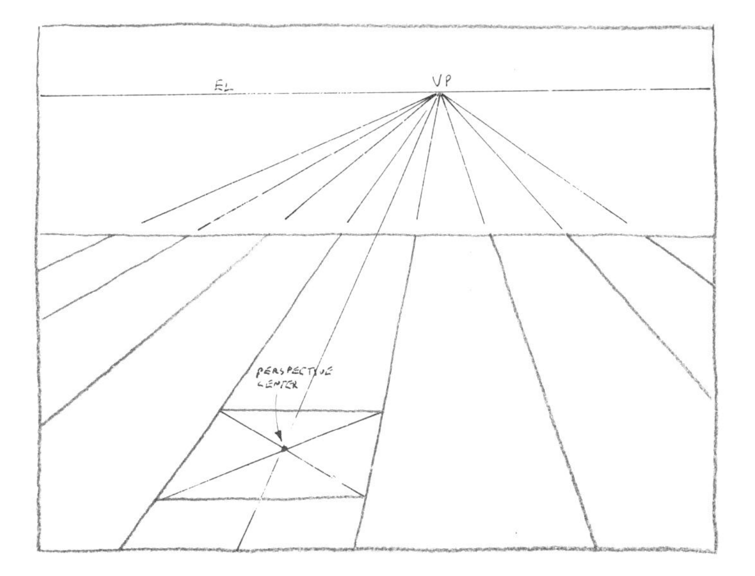

Draw a line from one end of the near tile edge through the "midpoint" of the far tile edge. Where that line hits line *a*, draw horizontal line *b*.

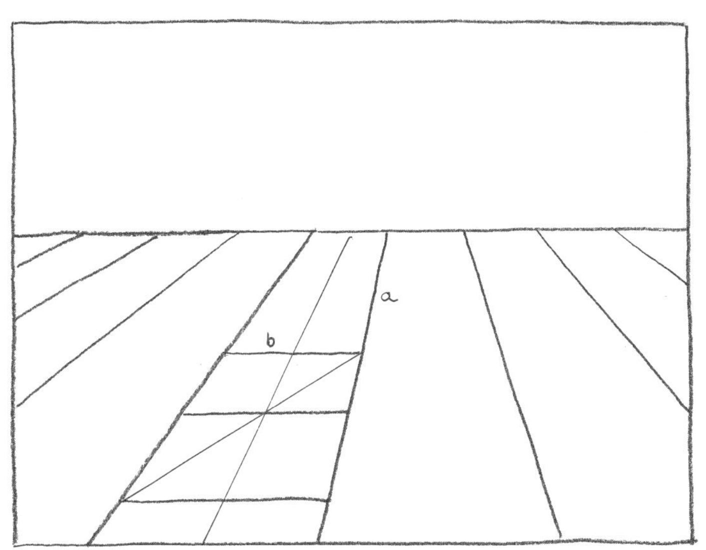

Continue this process until you hit the far wall. If the last tile doesn't come out exactly where the far wall begins, move the wall a little. Nobody will tell.

Beyond Eyeballing

Complete the floor. You can extend all the horizontal lines to the left and right, as shown here.

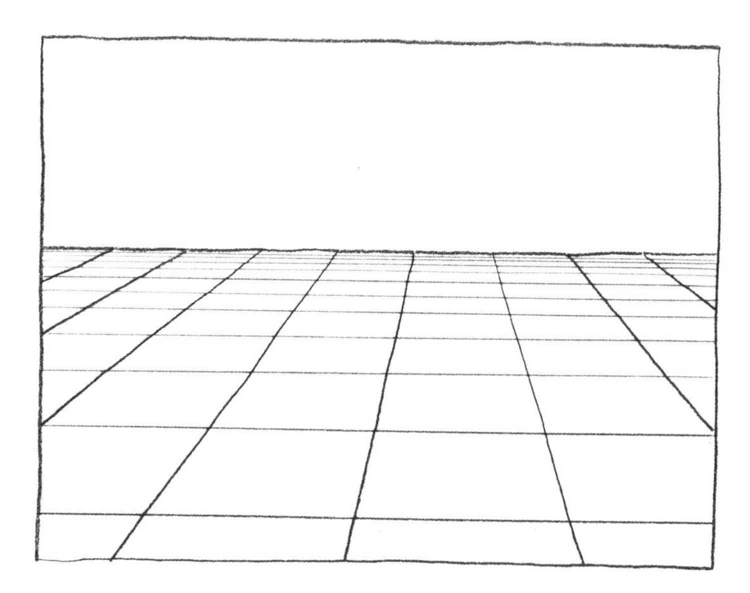

Or you can extend those lines only to alternating rows of tiles (if your floor is one with staggered joints) and draw another set of horizontal lines for the in-between rows of tiles.

Notice that line *m* isn't halfway between *p* and *q*—at least, not as the crow flies. It's halfway between *p* and *q* in perspective. To find instantly where that perspective midpoint is, cross the diagonals of the perspective square tile.

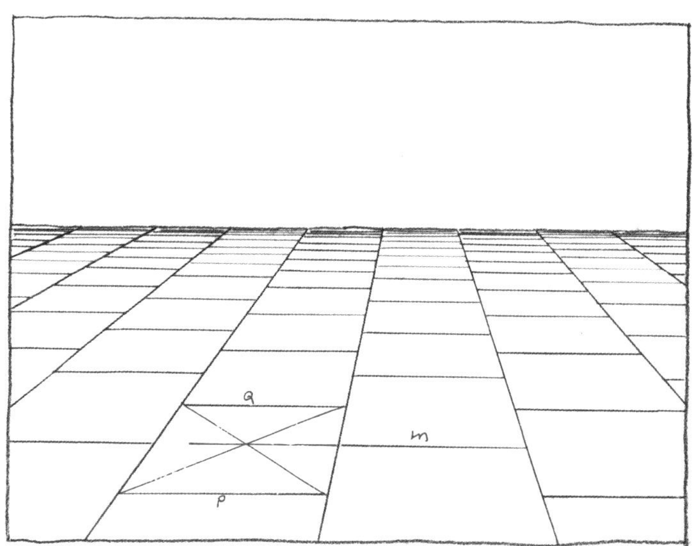

I mentioned earlier that in some instances you might want to use two-point perspective. You do everything the same except that you must draw the first two tile edges as slanting toward a second vanishing point (far to the left in my example, **right**), rather than draw them as horizontal lines. You'll see that if you give much slant to these lines your floor will feel as if it's tilted and running off the lower corner of your picture.

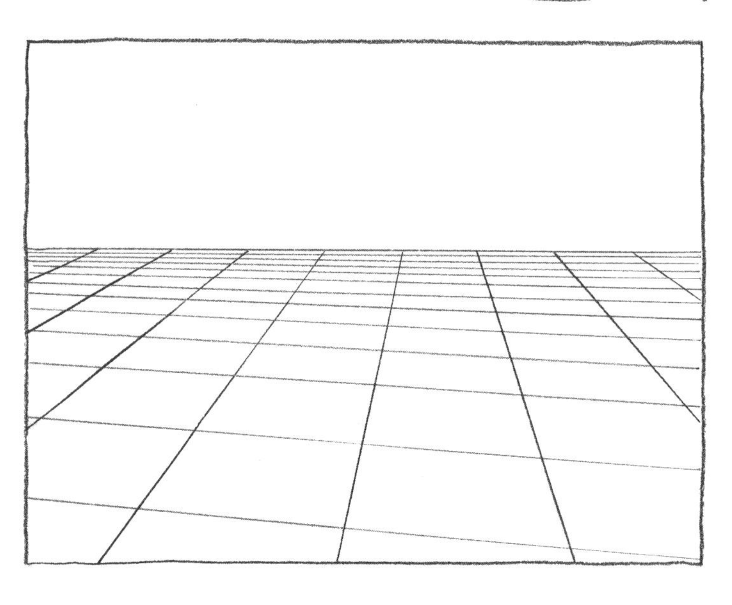

Exercise 6/**Spacing Objects Evenly in Perspective**

Here's a straight country road with utility poles on one side and fence posts on the other. The road is made of equal concrete sections. Draw the remaining posts, poles, and sections. The concrete sections can be drawn using the method in the text for tile floors. I've given you a second post to start them off; decide for yourself how much distance you want between poles and how long the concrete sections are to be. Note that I've indicated the two vanishing points on the horizon.

Placing People Properly

You might think people could be treated the same as any other objects in a drawing, and in some ways that's true. But because we observe people all the time we have a built-in, unconscious understanding of how they should look, and any liberties we take in drawing them in a scene are almost certain to be noticed. We can fudge the size or shape or position of a barn and get away with it, but if we take too many similar liberties with people, the results are usually all too obvious. Here are some general ideas about including people in a scene in proper perspective.

Scale

It's important to place people so that they seem in scale with their surroundings. The guy at **top right** looks as though he's about to embrace the utility pole.

But actually he's only waiting for the damsel to rush into his arms, **bottom right**.

There are two things wrong with this picture. First, the male figure is placed awkwardly next to the pole; second, either he's pretty tall or the pole is awfully short—there's something wrong with the scale, or proportions, between the two objects.

The first problem is easily resolved by leaving more space between the man and the pole. However, you might argue with my second point, saying that the pole is in the distance and that's why it looks so short. But if the pole were far enough in the distance to make its *height* plausible, it would be too *thick;* at that distance it should look slimmer. There's no way it could look almost as thick as a man—even a skinny man wasted away by love!

The simplest way to avoid placing figures awkwardly is to compare their heights with other objects that are as far back in the picture as they. Start with the knowledge that most people are five to six feet tall. Then observe how high some common things are: many rooms have ceilings eight feet high; a common doorway height is a few inches less than seven feet; a kitchen counter is about three feet; and so on. Get the height of one object the way you want it and fix the heights of all other objects (including people) relative to the object you started with.

If you have a mix of people, say adults and children, you have to rely a lot on clues other than height to signal what's going on. If, for example, the dress and the proportions of one figure clearly say "child," then that figure will not seem awkwardly placed next to a taller figure who clearly is an adult.

Placing People Properly

Eye Level

Whether you're painting barns or people or both, the eye level you establish for your picture is critical. Once you've established the eye level from which your scene is to be painted, all the objects (including people) in your picture must relate to that eye level. Let's consider a couple of examples of scenes with people.

First, suppose your scene is some flat area, such as a beach or a city square or practically anywhere in Indiana. Assume you're painting the scene standing at your easel. If you're an "average" person, your eyes are roughly five feet from the ground, so the eye level in your painting is five feet from the ground. So are the eye levels of all those average people in your painting. In other words, everybody in the scene who is of average height will have his eyes on the same level, five feet above the ground, as shown **top**.

What about the little twerp at the left? This figure is clearly a child, not just some adult off in the distance. How do we know that? Because, given a flat area like this, all standing adults have the same eye level. There's no way this little guy can be a regular adult and not have his eye level at the same height as everyone else's eye level.

A receding row of people along a flat area will diligently obey the "rules" of linear perspective, the same as pickets in a fence or poles along a road. That is, if you draw guidelines from the top and bottom of any of the figures in the sketch to any vanishing point on the eye level, you can fit as many other similar figures as you wish in between those two guidelines and they'll look right.

I've drawn in one pair of guidelines **bottom**—you draw in some others. Then sketch some people (five-foot-eye-level people) anywhere you wish between those pairs of lines and they'll look right. Try it. Don't forget to make the more distant figures skinnier and, of course, less detailed than nearer ones, in keeping with perspective techniques we've already discussed.

Suppose you wanted to add more children to this sketch. Remember that they are *below* your eye level. If a child is as far back in the scene as some adult, what the two will have in common is not their eye levels, but rather their feet level. If an adult and child are side by side, their *feet* will be on the same level (unless one of them is floating). So start with the feet and draw the child from the feet up.

Adjust children's heights relative to the heights of those around them. Once you get one child where you want him, you can add others in perspective, farther back or nearer, by drawing a pair of guidelines from the top and bottom of the established child to a vanishing point, just as we did with the adults. Then fit as many children as you want between those guidelines and you'll have a bunch of same-height children in proper perspective. If you want to practice a little more on this sketch, draw guidelines from the top and bottom of the child at the left to a vanishing point on the eye level, and fit some children between those guidelines.

Placing People Properly

Suppose the scene you're depicting is not flat. There may be some people in the picture whose eyes are at the picture's eye level, some above, and some below, as in this sketch.

What you must rely on here, other than careful observation, are techniques such as these:

- *Size variation:* Show a plausible size difference between near and distant people; measure their relative heights with thumb and pencil.
- *Detail:* Show less detail in figures farther away. Compare the figures on the hill to the one carrying the basket.
- *Overlap:* A couple of the figures have their legs "cut off" because the hill overlaps them. This visually pushes the figures back into the distance behind the hill.
- *Scale:* Establish scale by placing figures near objects whose sizes are generally understood by most viewers, such as the beach umbrella at the right in the sketch.
- *Visual clues:* Give the viewer hints about what's going on. For example, if a figure is meant to be below eye level, give some clues to prove it. In the sketch the figure carrying the basket and umbrella is below eye level (the ocean horizon off in the distance), and I have tried to underscore that fact not only by where I placed him, but by simple clues: you're looking slightly *down* into the basket he's holding; you're looking *down* on his hat, not seeing up beneath it.

Shadows

In several sections of these workbooks we have discussed the importance of shadows in enhancing the feeling of depth in a picture. In Workbook 1, for example, we discussed the type of shadow that hints at depth by helping to describe the thickness of an object. Remember the apple illustration? I first presented an apple as a flat shape that had no apparent thickness, or depth.

But as soon as I added shadow to the side of the apple away from the light source it became a three-dimensional object, no longer flat. That type of shadow, the shadow occurring on the side(s) of an object opposite the light source, is generally called *modeling.*

Later I introduced another type of shadow called *cast shadow.* A cast shadow is an area on any surface that is darker than the surrounding area because light is blocked and prevented from reaching it. Again going back to the apple in Workbook 1, both types of shadow are present—the shadow on the half of the apple away from the light source (modeling), and the shadow on the table surface caused by the apple blocking the light (cast shadow). We know intuitively that the cast shadow we see could not exist if there were not an object of some thickness blocking the light. So both types of shadow aid in promoting the feeling of depth in an indirect but vital way: by suggesting the thickness, or third dimension, of an object.

Another way in which shadows, especially cast shadows, add dimension to a picture is by telling the viewer about shapes and thicknesses he or she might otherwise not see. Earlier in this workbook, for example, I mentioned the importance of such details as the thickness of bricks or the overlapping of house siding. It's often because of cast shadows that the viewer is even aware of such details. Cast shadows help define shapes because wherever they fall they must follow the contours of the areas they are falling upon.

Because shadows can be so helpful in getting depth in a picture, it's important to understand what makes them tick. The following sections should shed some light on shadows.

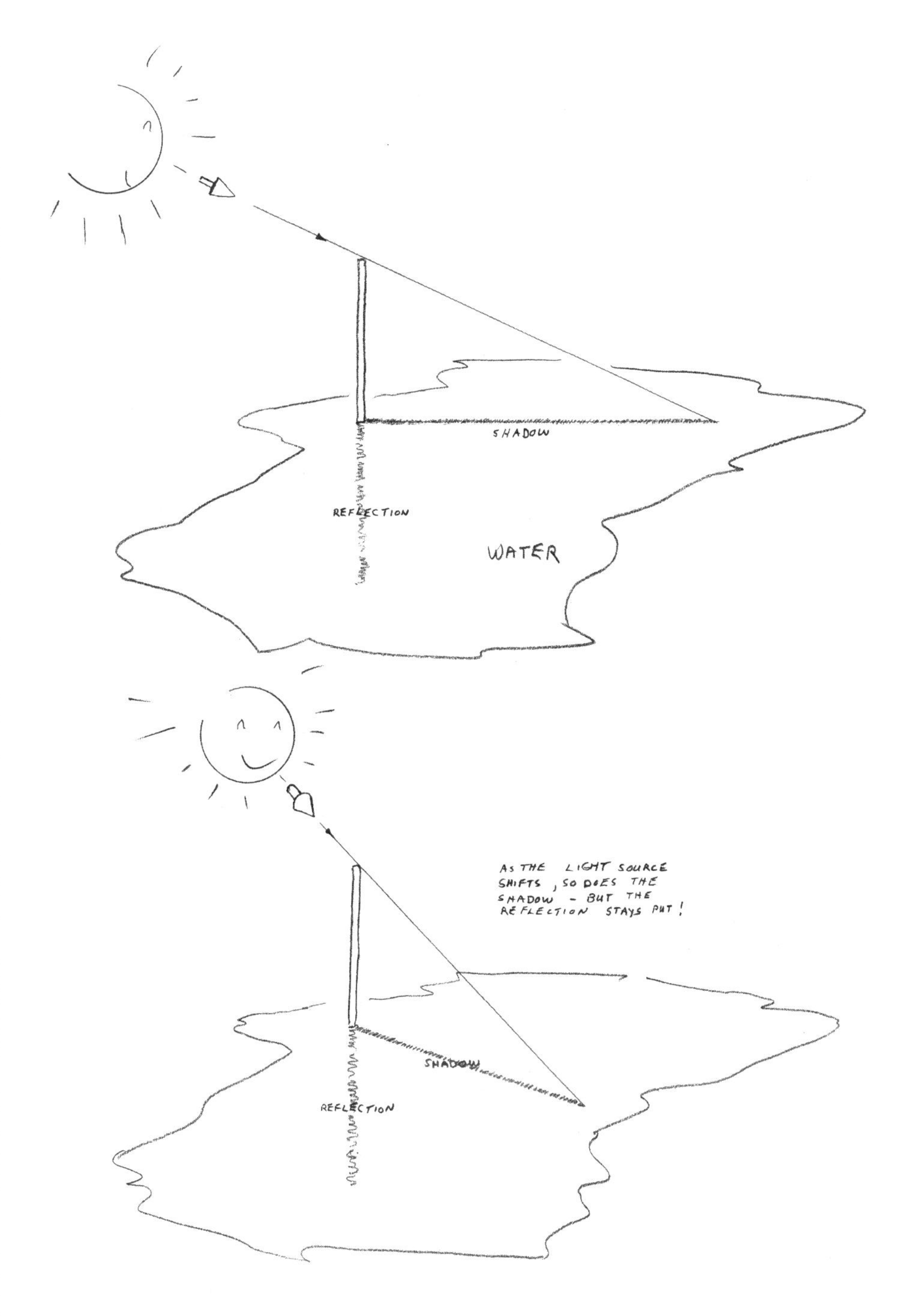

Shadows Are Not Reflections

There is often confusion between shadows and reflections. We'll get to reflections in the next section, but for now remember: a *shadow* is an area receiving less light than other areas because something is blocking the light; a *reflection* is an image you see caused by light from an object bouncing from some surface and reaching your eye.

In the **top** sketch, the light source (sun) is at the left. Its rays get to everything except the area blocked by the pole. That area is the pole's shadow. The reflection seen in the water is caused by light traveling from the pole, hitting the mirrorlike surface of the water, and bouncing up to be seen by the eyes of the observer.

If we shift the position of the light source (the sun), say by moving it back some behind the pole, the position of the shadow changes but the reflection remains the same, **bottom**.

Shadows

Multiple vs. Single Shadows

If you have a single light source, you get a single cast shadow; with two light sources you get two shadows, **right**.

In fact, theoretically there could be as many shadows as there are light sources. This doesn't quite work out in reality, however, because the area the shadows are cast on eventually becomes so awash with light from all those sources that no shadows at all are discernible. Still, it's not uncommon to have two, three, or four sources. When painting a still life indoors, for example, there could be light from a window (sunlight) and light from a couple of different lamps. It's important to decide in such cases whether you want (a) multiple light sources and the multiple shadows they cause, or (b) a single light source and single shadows. The former is more natural and may give your subject a more ordinary look; the latter offers a more dramatic "spotlighted" look.

One of the effects of multiple light sources is to make shadows less dark, because the light from each source invades the shadow caused by the other source. A second effect is that the edges of the shadows will be less sharp.

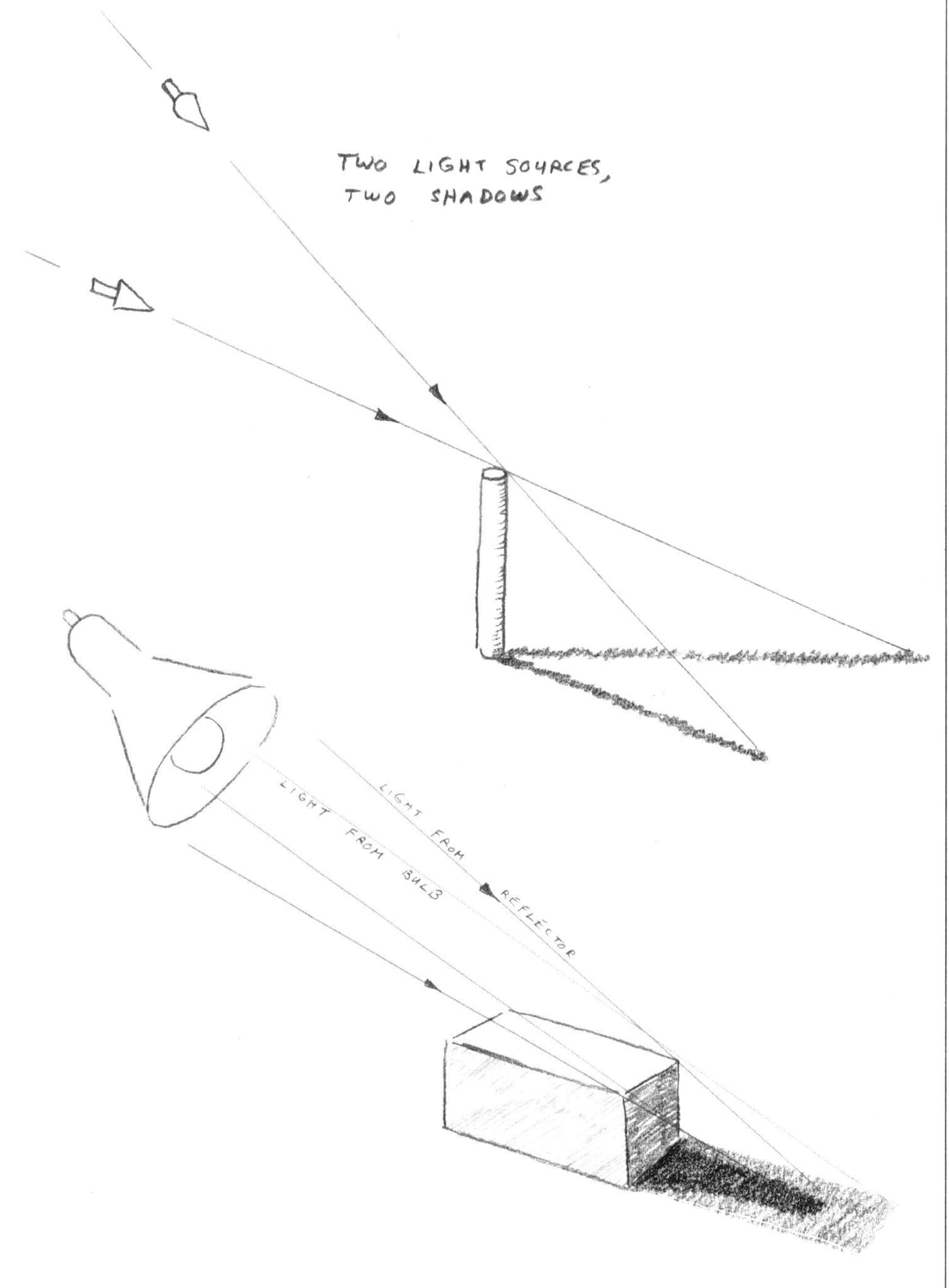

Notice in the sketch **above** that the area where the two shadows overlap is darker than the rest of the shadows. That's because light doesn't get to this area from either source.

While checking up on my own understanding of shadows by playing with the lights at my desk, I rediscovered something I had almost forgotten: a "single" light source can give you a multiple shadow. Here's the arrangement I have in front of me. What I get is two shadows, a darker inner one and a lighter outer one.

What's happening is this: The bulb is one light source and the light rays from it alone would give me a single shadow, but the reflector around the bulb is also sending out light rays. Some of the light from the reflector is coming at the block from a wider angle than the rays from the bulb, and those rays get past the block and fall within the original shadow area, lightening that area wherever they fall.

Shadows

Figuring Them Out

Sometimes it's difficult to figure out how a shadow from a given object would fall over a particular surface. Clearly, the best way to get a shadow right is to photograph the subject when the shadows are where you want them. Then, despite the sun's shifting in the sky or your children's shifting of your lamp, you can refer to the photograph. That's not cheating, just smart.

When all else fails, I have resorted to the dark-room-and-flashlight method. It's patented, but I'll share it with you. Set up something roughly similar to the thing you're trying to understand, darken the room, and use a flashlight as a "sun." (Obviously, if what you're working on is a still life, this is all unnecessary—you simply look at the still life and see how the shadows are behaving.)

As an example, suppose you want to see what sort of shadow a tree trunk will cast on a brick wall with recessed mortar joints. Sounds simple, I know, but just which way *does* the shadow go when it gets into those recessed joints?

Find a few fat books and a few thin ones and pile them up. The fat books are bricks, the skinny ones are mortar joints.

Now turn out the lights (no fooling around!) and hold the flashlight behind a stick or ruler representing the tree trunk, and you'll have an immediate and unequivocal answer to your question, **below left**. (By the way, the flashlight has the same problem as the lamp I discussed above. Its reflector causes multiple shadows. Hold it as far behind the stick as you can reach to get sharper shadows.)

There's Stuff in There

Look into any shadow and what do you see? Certainly not total blackness, which is the way shadows are often painted. Peer intently into a shadowed area, and you'll find a lot going on there. Perhaps the first thing you'll notice is some rich color. Whatever color is there in the shadowed object may well look more intense than if the shadow were absent, because you're seeing it relative to all that darkness. The next thing you'll notice is that you can find an extraordinary amount of detail in the shadow—detail that might be lost or washed out in the full glare of sunlight. Another common discovery is that the shadow is by no means uniform in darkness, or value.

The final thing to pay attention to is the nature of the edges of a shadow. Shadows cast in sunlight tend to be sharp, since the sun is a single light source not surrounded by an annoying lamp reflector. Yet the edges you see on shadows outdoors are not always crisp. The edges will be softened if the shadow is falling over some textured area, such as a lawn or hayfield, as opposed to a smooth concrete highway. They may also be softened by strong light bouncing into the shadow from nearby objects, such as bright, white buildings. If you paint shadows too rigidly, too sharply, they'll look pasted-on and unnatural.

Shadows Obey the Law

Most often the cast shadows we draw are rather irregular shapes cast on irregular surfaces by irregular objects, so the best you can do is observe the shadows' shapes and draw them the way you see them. But to help you understand the irregular shapes you see, let's study what happens in an orderly situation such as the one **below center**.

What we have is a neat cube in one-point perspective casting a neat shadow on a flat surface. The thing to notice here is that the edges of such shadows obey the rules of perspective. In this case, for example, the outer edge of the shadow recedes to the same vanishing point as the edges of the cube.

In the next example, **below right**, the shadow cast by the sphere would be circular, if you could view it from directly above. But in keeping with our knowledge of perspective, this circle seen from the side is an ellipse.

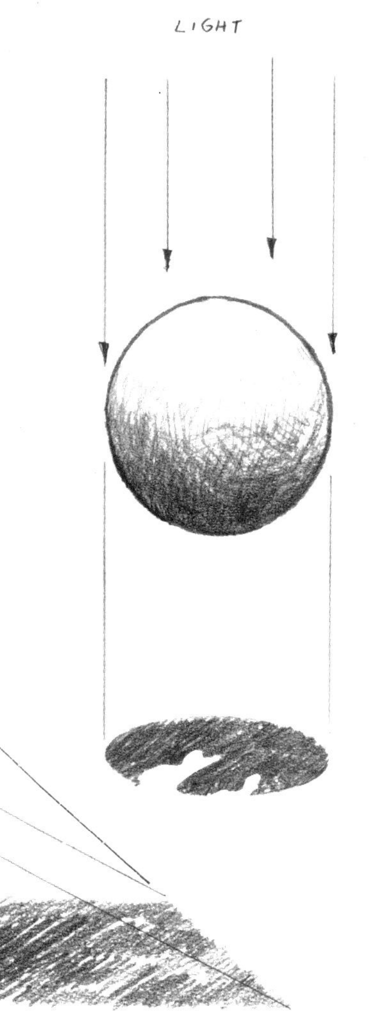

Exercise 7/**Shadows**

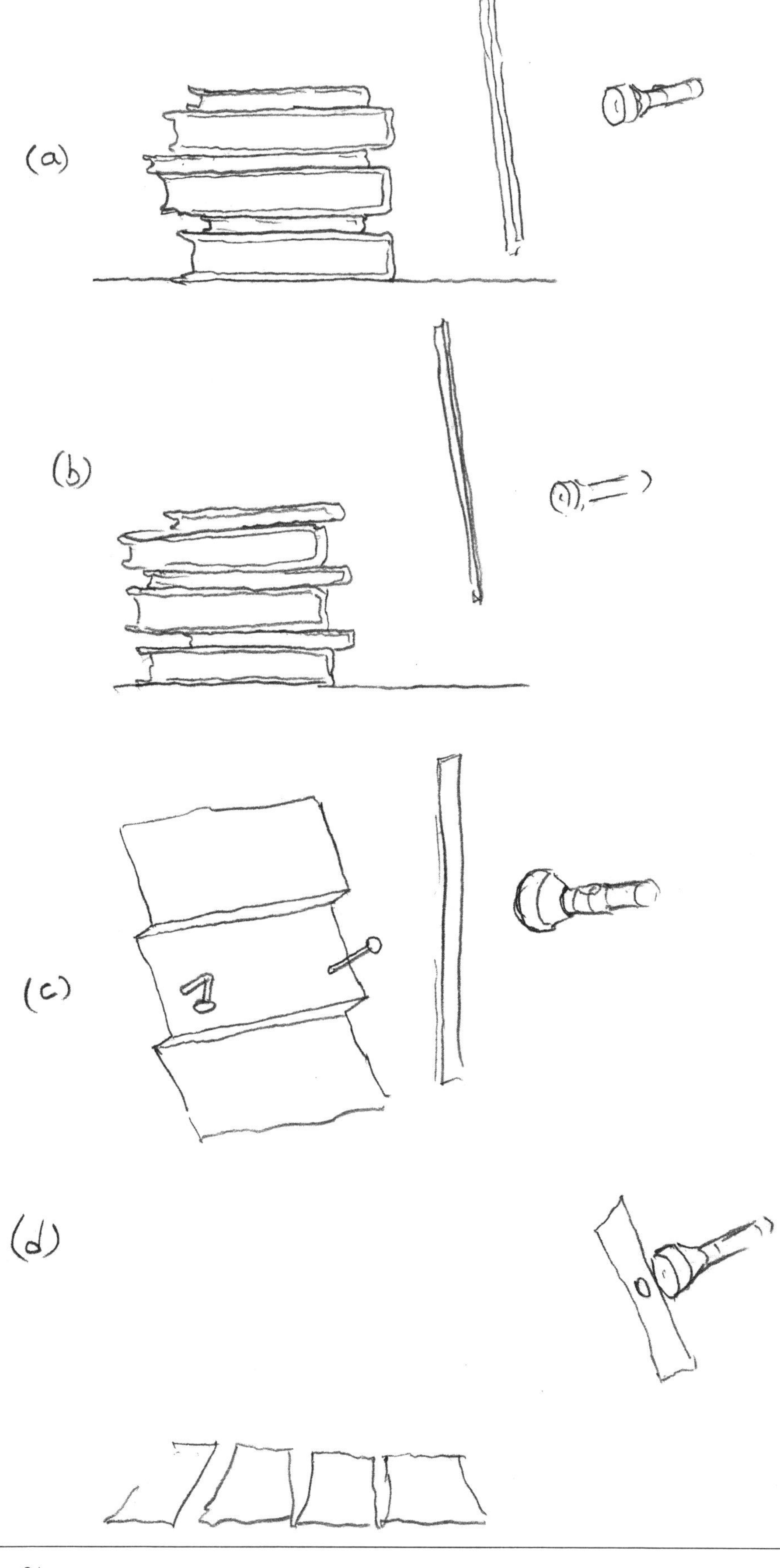

Let's play in the dark. You'll need a flashlight, some books, and a piece of stiff paper or light cardboard. The problem is to simulate in your studio some conditions you're not sure of concerning shadows.

A. Stack three or so fat books and the same number of thinner ones in alternating fashion, letting the thick ones stick out beyond the thin ones. Using your flashlight and a yardstick, cast shadows on this simulated brick wall from the left, from the right, and straight ahead. Make notes to remind you how the shadows look as they jump the indented "mortar joints." Also move the flashlight higher and lower and see what effect this has, especially on the shadows cast by the edges of the "bricks."

B. Repeat A, but this time have protruding "mortar joints." Note what happens to the shadows when they hit a bulging mortar joint.

C. Fold a piece of stiff paper or light cardboard in the shape of board siding. Cast shadows over the siding using the flashlight and yardstick in many positions. Stick a small nail part way into the "siding" and note its shadow. Then use a bent nail and watch how its shadow performs.

D. You can leave the lights on for this one. Lay out a succession of materials of differing values (lightness and darkness) and differing textures—for example, a strip of smooth white paper, a strip of black or gray paper, a piece of terrycloth towel. Use your flashlight or a lamp to cast a shadow simultaneously over all these materials, and notice the differences in apparent darkness of the shadow as it passes over each material and the crispness of the edge of the shadow on smooth versus textured materials. To get a better simulation of sunlight and avoid the "double" shadows the flashlight will give you, cut a one-inch round hole in a piece of cardboard and hold it in front of the flashlight so that only light directly from the bulb gets through.

Reflections

We see an object because light travels from that object to our eyes. We see a *reflection* of an object because light travels from the object to a relatively smooth surface and bounces from that surface toward our eyes.

All that's necessary in order to see a reflection of an object is that there be some reflecting surface, such as water, situated at the right distance between you and the object. There must obviously be some source of light in order for anything to be seen, but the *position* of the light source has nothing to do with the reflection's position. Move the sun anywhere you want and the reflection will stay put.

There is a rule in physics that governs reflections, but it's an easy one that even we absent-minded painters can understand and retain. Formally stated, the rule is this:

The angle of incidence equals the angle of reflection.

Or, when light whacks a smooth surface and bounces off, it bounces off at the same angle at which it whacked it, as shown at **top**. Always. It never bounces as in the **center** drawing.

These diagrams show only a single ray of light coming from the tree. Actually, there are rays of light coming from every single tiny bit of the tree and they radiate in all directions. But the rays in which we're interested are only those which strike the water surface at just the right place so that their bounce will take them directly to the viewer's eye. Billions of rays manage to behave and make it to the viewer, and the viewer sees a complete tree stretched across the water.

If you drive a car, you're familiar with another example of how reflections behave. When you glance into your rearview mirror to watch what's going on behind you, you're taking advantage of the rule we stated above. Light entering your rear window from whatever is behind your car strikes your mirror and bounces off the mirror toward your eyes, **bottom left**.

That is, it does if your mirror is tilted properly. If it's not, you of course adjust it. What you're doing is steering the light so that it will reach your eyes rather than bounce off somewhere else. If the mirror is twisted too far toward you, then the image from behind you gets lost, **bottom right**.

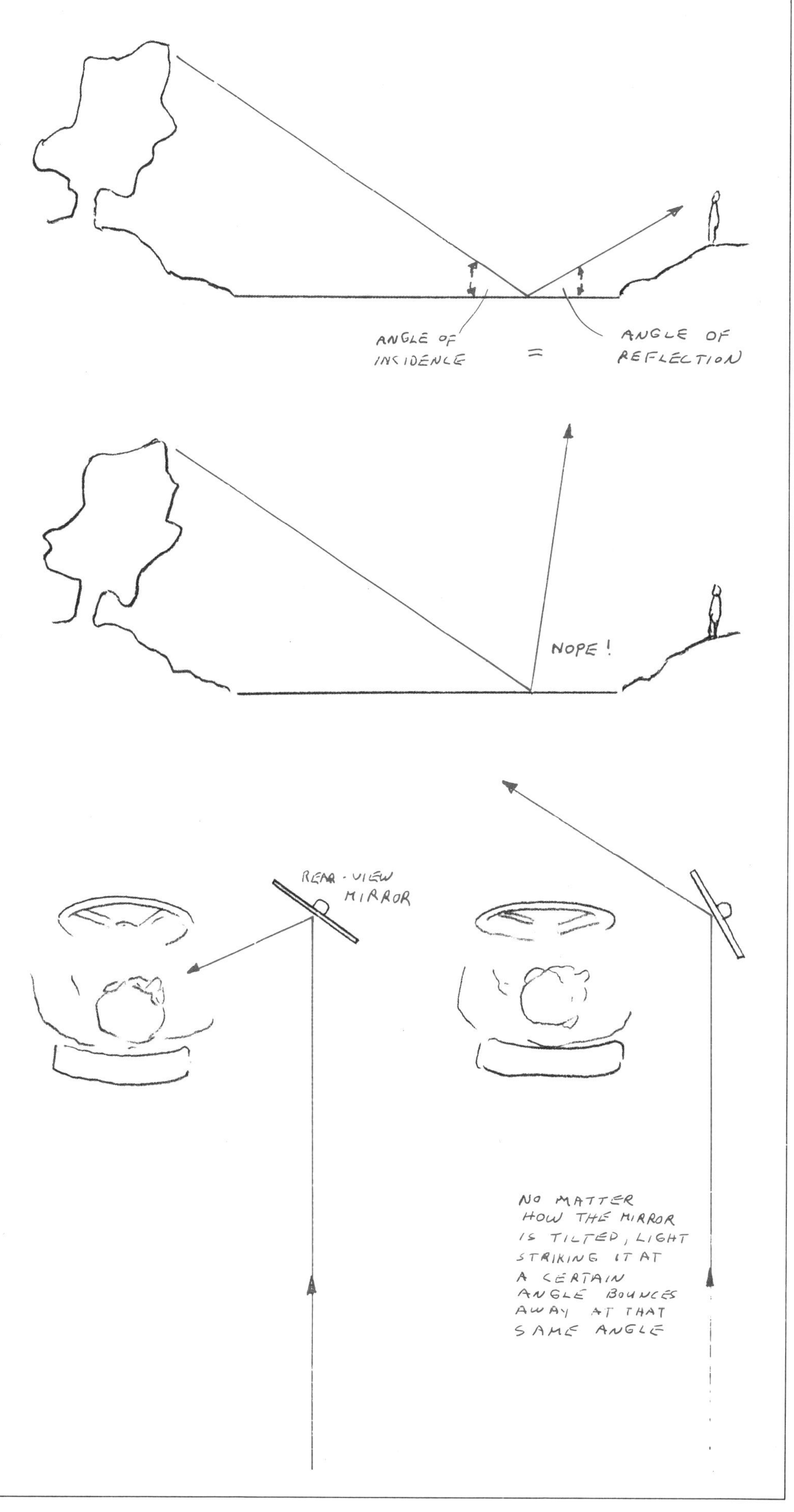

Reflections

Deportment

A reflection behaves very well. It's always predictable. If you see a reflection of a vertical object stretching across a pond, it always aims right toward you. A friend off to your left or right will see the same object reflected, but the reflection he sees will aim right toward him. No two people see precisely the same reflection. A reflection, after all, is defined by the light that makes its way to *your* eyes.

If an object is not vertical, some important and still totally predictable things happen to its reflection. Suppose you're looking at a lone piling sticking out of the water. Depending on whether it's vertical or leaning, you'll see one of the reflections shown at **near right**.

How about a piling leaning toward you or away from you? In the previous example, the reflection was the same size as the piling. Here, however, the reflection appears shorter than the piling as the piling tilts away from you and longer when the piling tilts toward you, **far right**.

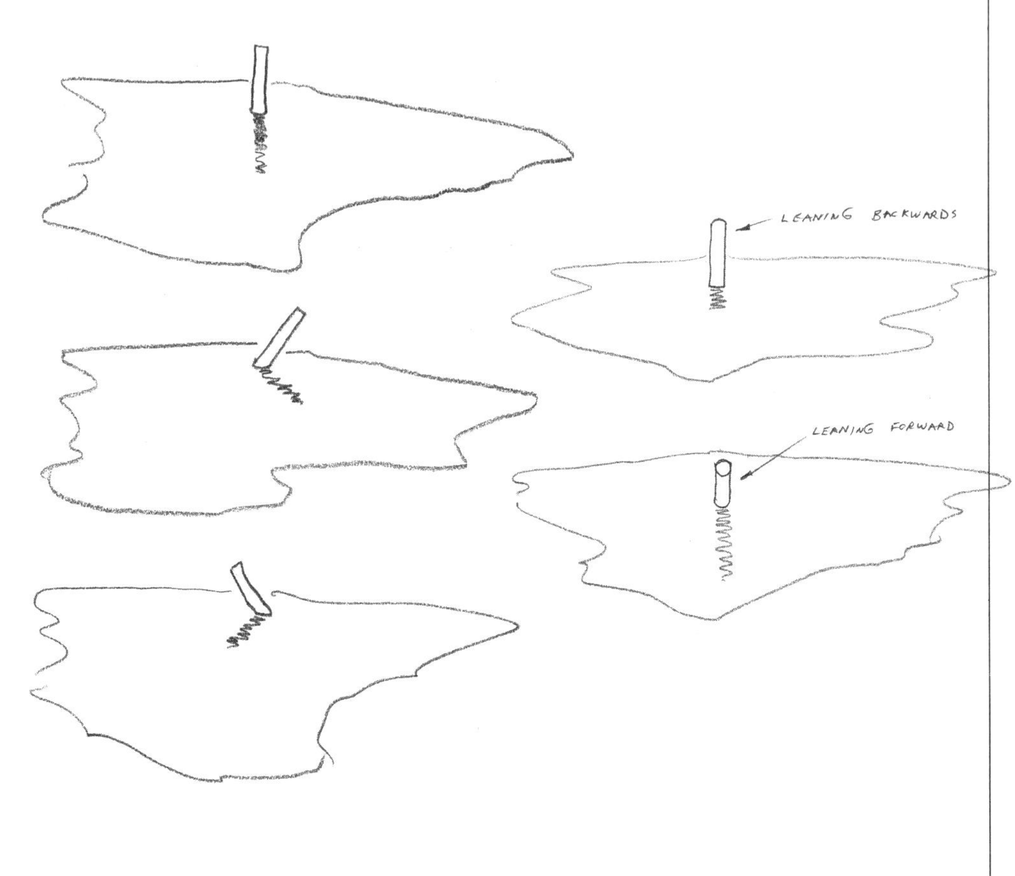

Exercise 8/**Reflections**

Lay a flat mirror face up on the table to simulate a pond. It's best to have a mirror at least two feet square or so, but a smaller one will work. If you have no flat mirror you can easily make one for our purposes by laying a piece of clean Plexiglas or similar rigid glazing over a piece of black matboard.

A. Set up various objects at the edge of your simulated pond and view them from across the pond. Something like a large marker will do well. First stand the marker on end, vertically, and notice that the reflection is about as long as the marker. Tilt the marker to the right and to the left and see which way the reflection goes. Now tilt the marker toward you and watch the relative lengths of the marker and its reflection. Do the same tilting the marker away from you. Try combinations of tilts, such as away and to the right.

B. Set the marker vertically at the far edge of the mirror. Get comfortable in a position where you can see its reflection stretched out across the "pond" toward you. Don't move. Have a friend lay a small object (a tack, perhaps) at the end of the reflection nearest you. Your friend won't be seeing the same reflection as you, so you'll have to guide him or her in placing the tack. When the tack is in place at the end of the reflection *as you see it,* get up and stand over the mirror and prepare for a surprise. That reflection you saw as quite short actually stretched a long way across your "pond"!

C. Set the marker anywhere on the mirror. Lay a piece of white paper alongside it and turn out the room lights. Shine a flashlight on the marker so that the marker casts a shadow on the paper (the paper is only there because it makes the shadow easier to see). Move the flashlight as if it were the sun in the sky and watch how both the direction and length of the shadow change, but notice that the REFLECTION NEVER CHANGES as long as you keep your head in the same place. (This may be easier to do with someone else moving the light for you.) Keep moving the flashlight and notice that there is only one position at which the reflection and the shadow happen to coincide—that's when the light is directly behind the marker, so that you and the light source and the marker all line up.

The exercise proves that what I said would happen does happen, but it doesn't explain why. Understanding the "why" involves some geometry which is really not too relevant here. As a painter, all you'll need is to have a good general understanding of how and why things happen and then to rely on observation to resolve particular problems.

It's fairly common in landscape painting for reflections to be the same size as the objects being reflected. In cases where there seems to be a departure from this general rule, you have two tools to rely on for getting things right: (1) Always "measure" what you see before you, using the pencil-and-thumb method, and trust in your measurements; (2) When in doubt (for example, when you're dreaming up a scene rather than painting from an actual situation) set up a reflecting surface, such as a flat mirror, and test out what happens.

Broken Reflections

I just finished telling you that reflections will usually be the same size as the objects being reflected. However, there are important exceptions to this "rule." Have you ever wondered why we see a moon's reflection stretching across miles of water? Or why we see long reflections of automobile taillights in the street on a rainy night? Or why we see tree reflections stretching all the way across a lake on a breezy day?

Vertical objects and their reflections are the same size *if the reflecting surface is relatively smooth*—a mirror, for example, or a shiny desk top, or a calm body of water. The ocean and the rainy road and the lake on a breezy day, however, are never smooth; they are imperfect reflectors. In all three cases we have not just a single, smooth, continuous surface, but a surface made up of zillions of tiny, curved reflectors.

If you could look at a cross section of a piece of pavement, for example, covered by a film of rainwater, it would look something like the drawing at **top right**.

Each of those tiny knobs of pavement covered with a film of water (and oil, probably) is a miniature curved mirror. Light rays from the object, let's say a taillight, strike all those teeny curved mirrors at lots of angles, **center**.

Some of those light rays are bound to hit a knob at such an angle that they will bounce in the direction of your eye (the angle of incidence equals the angle of reflection), while most will bounce elsewhere and be lost. But the effect is as though there were literally thousands of little mirrors stretching all the way from the taillight to your feet, each one tilted at just the right angle to bounce some light up to your eye.

The same thing happens if you're looking across a water surface that is at all rippled. Each little wavelet is a potential curved mirror, and many of them will succeed in reflecting light in your direction, **bottom**. You may have noticed on a moonlit night, if you were not being otherwise distracted, that not only does this fuzzy moon reflection come far across the water, but there are occasional flickers of reflections off to the side of the main beam. This happens whenever a wavelet is in just the right position to direct a moonbeam toward your eyes.

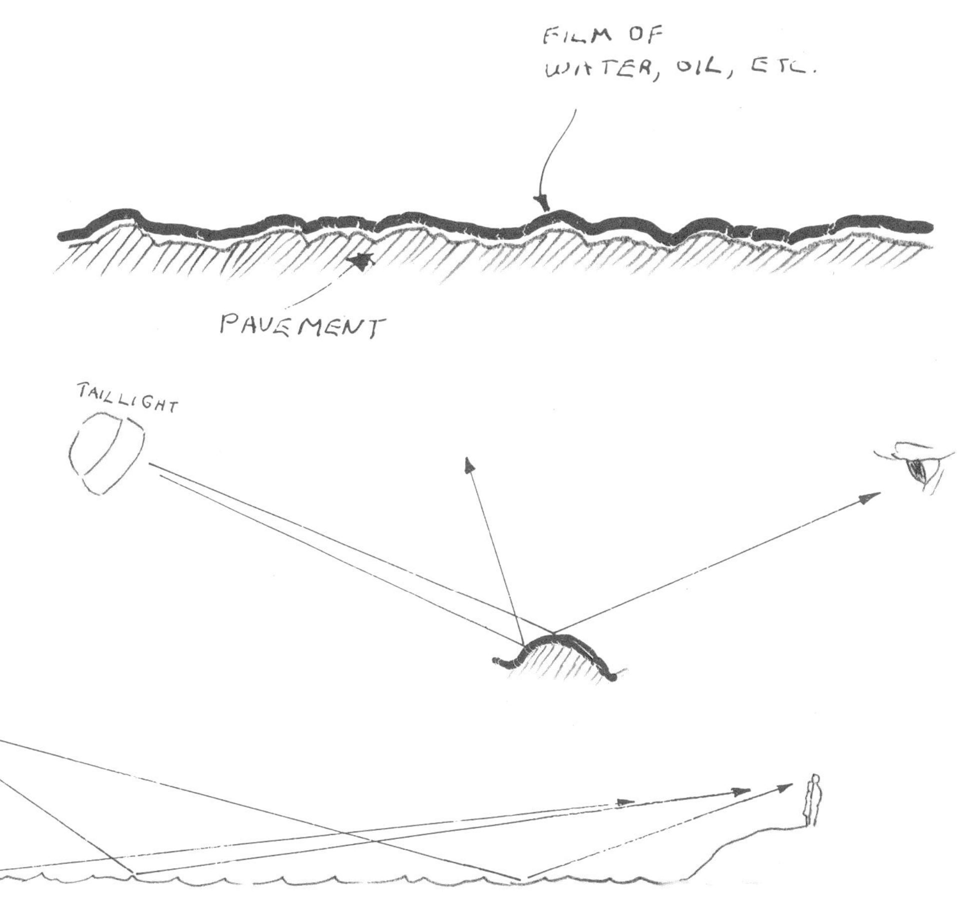

Exercise 9/**Broken Reflections**

We're going to simulate what happens to reflections on a rainy night. Turn on your flashlight and turn off the room lights. Lay the flashlight at the far edge of your mirror with the lit end facing you. Pretend it's a car's taillight. The mirror is the road surface. So far, if your mirror is reasonably clean, all you see is a crisp reflection of the taillight.

Now squirt some droplets from a spray bottle containing water, gin, or whatever onto the mirror between you and the flashlight. Don't squirt too hard and not directly at the mirror. Just let droplets settle onto the mirror, like raindrops falling on a road. The little droplets will act like a rough, water-covered road and will begin to disperse little broken light reflections. You'll notice the crisp reflection of the flashlight will gradually fade and a fuzzy reflection will stretch out toward you. Keep giving short squirts until this happens. This simulation won't be as dramatic as the real thing on a rainy night, but it'll give you a good idea what happens. The flashlight, of course, can represent the moon and the wet mirror, a lake. You could produce similar results with a pan of water. Have someone vibrate the pan enough to disturb the water surface and observe how the flashlight's reflection becomes broken.

Reflections

Effects of Distance

Sooner or later in your landscape painting the question will arise: how far back can this object be and still be seen as a reflection? In the sketch **below**, for instance, does it make a difference whether the hill is close to the edge of the water or far back?

It certainly does. For a given height hill, the farther back you move it, the shorter its reflection becomes. The two versions of this scene shown, **center**, are entirely plausible.

In (a) I've kept the hill the same height but moved it farther back into the distance. In (b) I've moved it so far back that it no longer reflects.

What happens in (b) is illustrated in the side view, **bottom**. Light from the hill cannot strike the water at such an angle as to reach the observer's eye.

What this means to you as an artist is that you can feel free to make objects either reflect or not, as you wish, simply by placing them far enough forward or back in the painting. If you decide you don't want the hill in my example to cause a reflection, simply leave it alone, and let it represent a faraway hill. Don't forget, however, to make it feel distant by using the appropriate perspective techniques, such as aerial perspective and blurred edges.

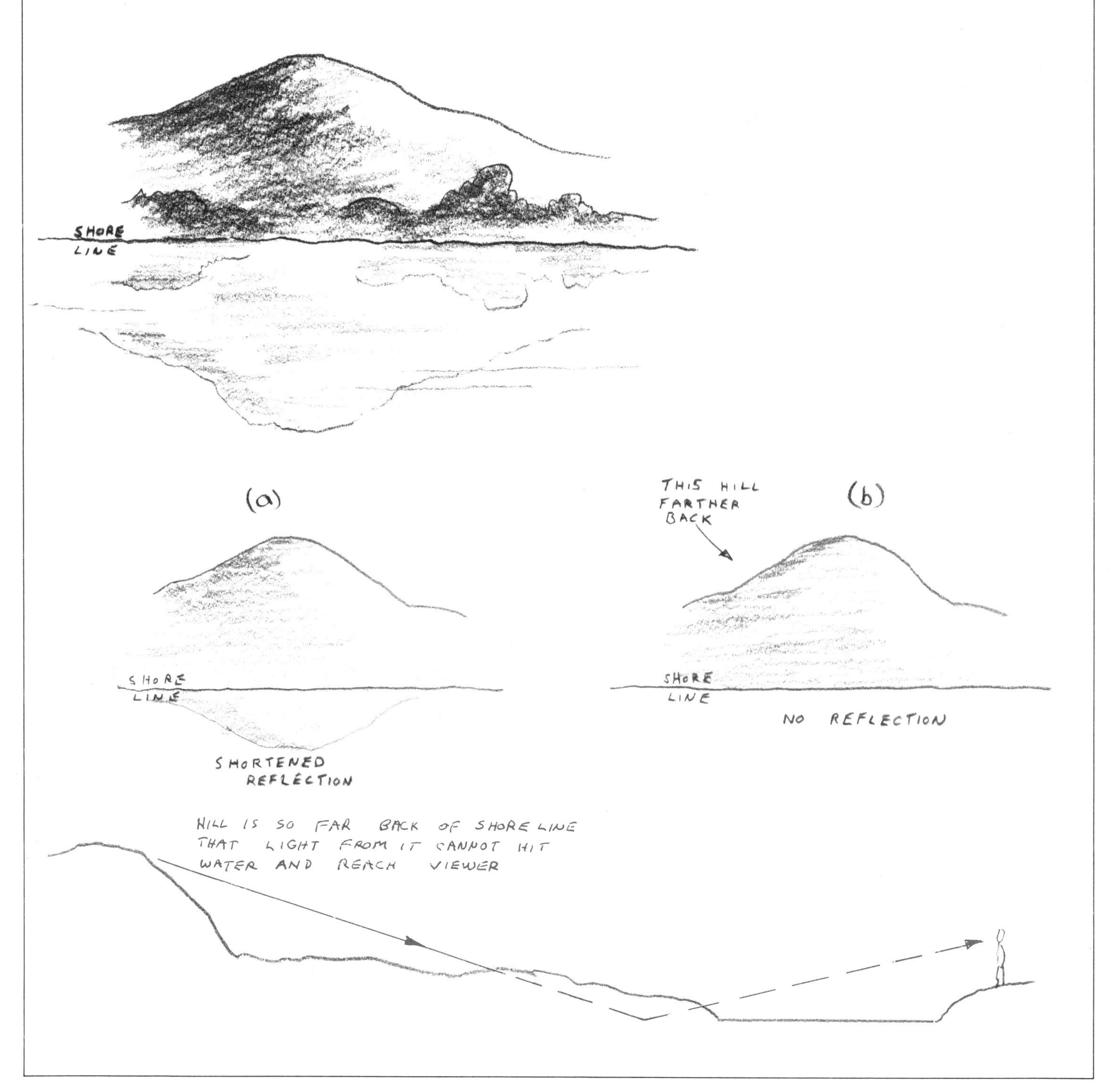

Exercise 10/**Reflecting Hidden Surfaces**

Read all instructions for Exercises 10 and 11 before cutting out house. If you want to avoid destroying what appears on the other side of this page, trace the template and transfer it to another piece of paper or cardboard.

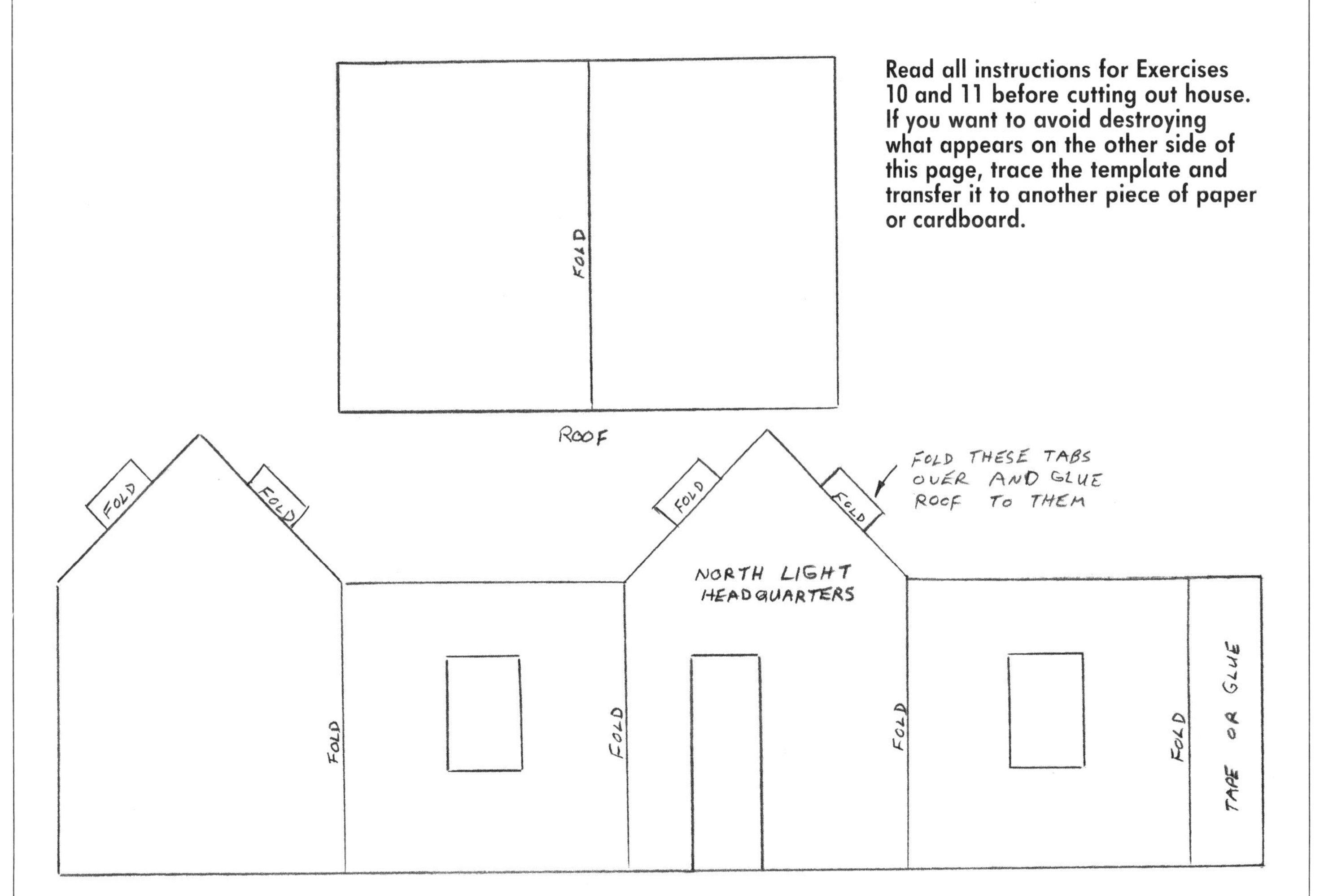

You can very often see parts of a structure in its reflection that are not visible in the structure itself. Build a little house from the template supplied. Glue or tape the base together and fasten the roof on. Then place the house at the edge of your mirror and view its reflection as you rotate the house through various positions. You'll see that in some positions the underside of the roof overhang is visible in the reflection even though all you see looking at the house itself is the outer surface of the roof. (Save the house for the next exercise.)

If you don't feel like making the house, simply pile up some books at the edge of the mirror, with the top books overlapping the bottom books in your direction. You'll see in the reflection the bottoms of those overlapping books.

Exercise 11/**Reflections and Distance**

Now we'll build a mountain and use it along with the house. Cut out the mountain and fold back the two ends so that it will stand up. Place your house at the far edge of the mirror. Put the mountain directly behind it, as if it were simply a hill right behind the house. Look at the reflections from across the pond. You'll see the reflection of the hill extending beyond the reflection of the house.

Now move the hill back gradually and watch as its reflection disappears behind the house. Finally, when you move the hill far enough back, it ceases to reflect at all. The importance of what you've seen is this: you can decide whether you want an object to reflect or not simply by moving it closer to or farther from the reflecting surface, without in any way altering its height.

Other Reflections

While a major portion of the reflections you encounter in landscape painting are on flat, horizontal surfaces, there are plenty of reflections in vertical surfaces, such as windows and shiny machinery, and indoors there are reflections in all kinds of glassware, metallic objects, tile, polished wood, and so on. Treatment of such reflections would require a workbook of its own, but I can offer you here a few things to watch for.

First, as always, paint what you see. There are no rules needed for that. But look carefully. You might be painting a rounded silver bowl, for example, and the reflections of objects both inside and outside the bowl, and find that some very strange (but geometrically predictable) things happen in the reflections. Sometimes the reflection is upside-down compared to the object, sometimes it's split into two reflections, and sometimes it's warped and almost shapeless. The size of the object and the size of the reflection may be markedly different. Stick your nose in there and see what those reflections are doing.

Second, simplify complicated reflections so that they don't take over the painting (unless, of course, reflections are really the subject of your painting). You usually don't need to paint a reflection literally—often a few well-placed blobs of color will do.

Third, if you're not sure what would happen under particular circumstances, fall back on tests such as those we performed in the preceding exercises. Simulate a condition you're not sure of.

Read all instructions for Exercises 10 and 11 before cutting out house. If you want to avoid destroying what appears on the other side of this page, trace the template and transfer it to another piece of paper or cardboard.

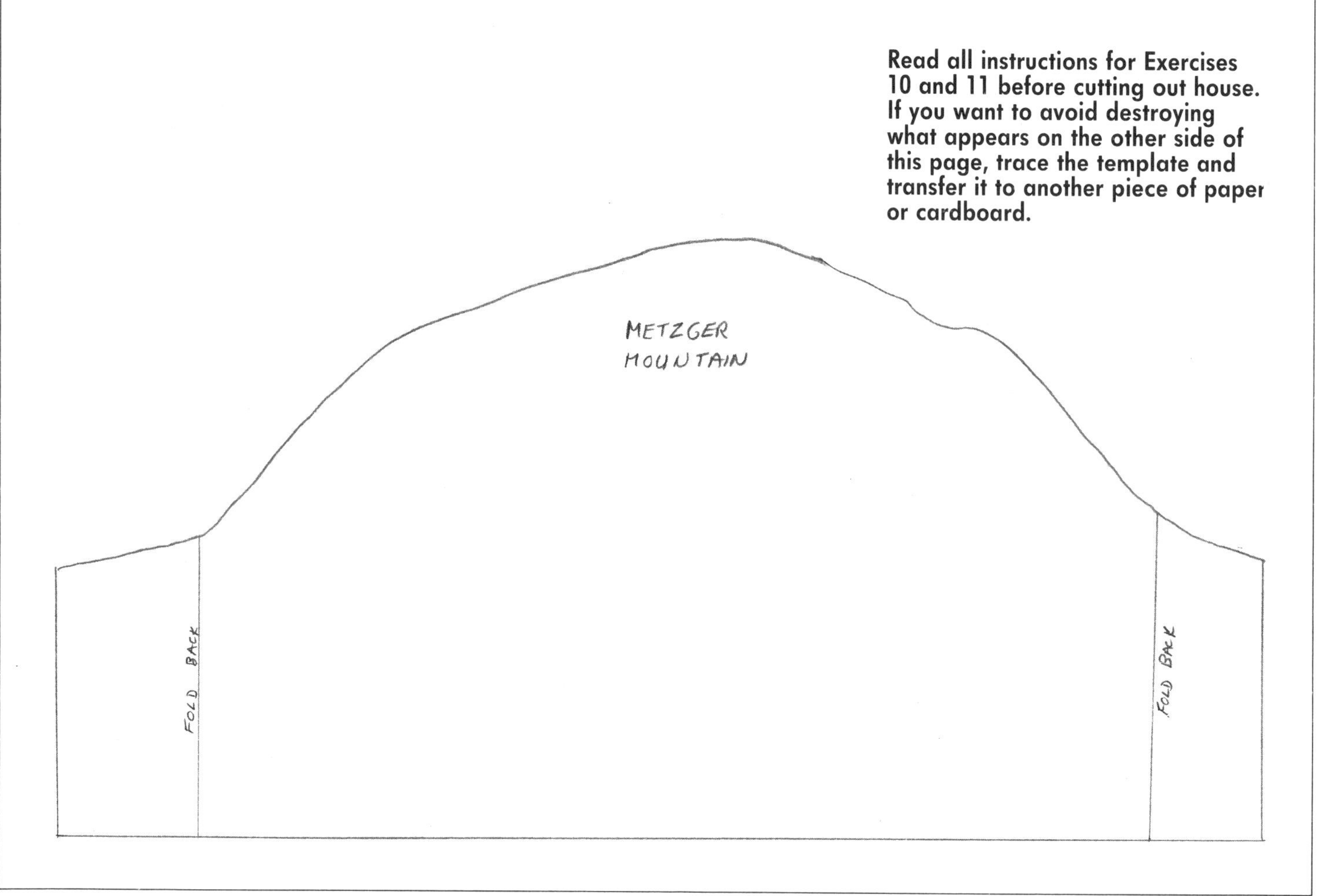

Refractions

I said in the last section that, for practical purposes, light can be considered to travel in a straight line. It can be "bent," however, when it leaves one medium, such as water, and enters another medium, such as air, at an angle. What happens is something like the diagram at **top right**.

The reason the shaft of light changes direction as it emerges from the water to the air is that it travels more slowly in the denser water than in air. I always picture the beam as doing a sort of little cartwheel as one side of the beam breaks through the surface of the "thick" water and finds freedom in the thin air. As soon as the entire beam is free in the air the light continues in its new straight-line direction.

An observer looking down at the fish in the sketch at **center right** will not see it where it really is, but where the dotted image is. As far as the observer's eye and brain are concerned, the light came from A, not from B. Our seeing apparatus accepts the light that enters the eye and interprets it as having traveled in a straight line.

What refraction means to most people is that you can't always trust what you see. If you shove a straight stick into some water, for example, you'll "see" a bent stick because of refraction. Go ahead, hold a pencil or a stick in a bowl of water and watch it bend.

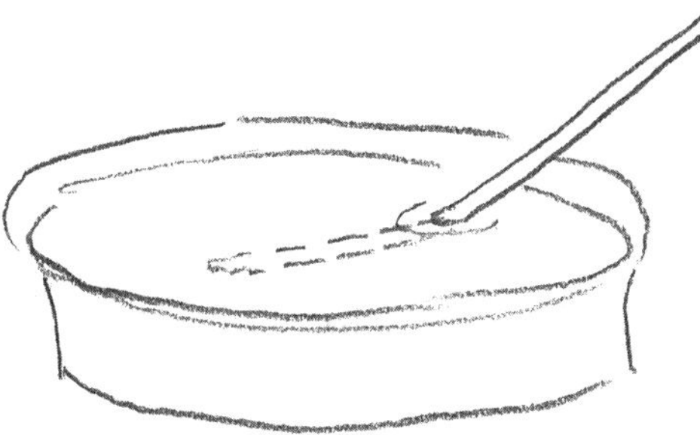

Or look at an object through a bottle or a glass. The sketch at **bottom right** shows how I see a marker through a decanter half-filled with water.

For a painter, refraction offers some visual delights, especially in painting glass objects. As in the case of my decanter, all kinds of devilish warps occur as light from an object passes through various combinations of air, glass, and liquids before reaching your eye. When painting such a subject, don't be afraid to paint what you see.

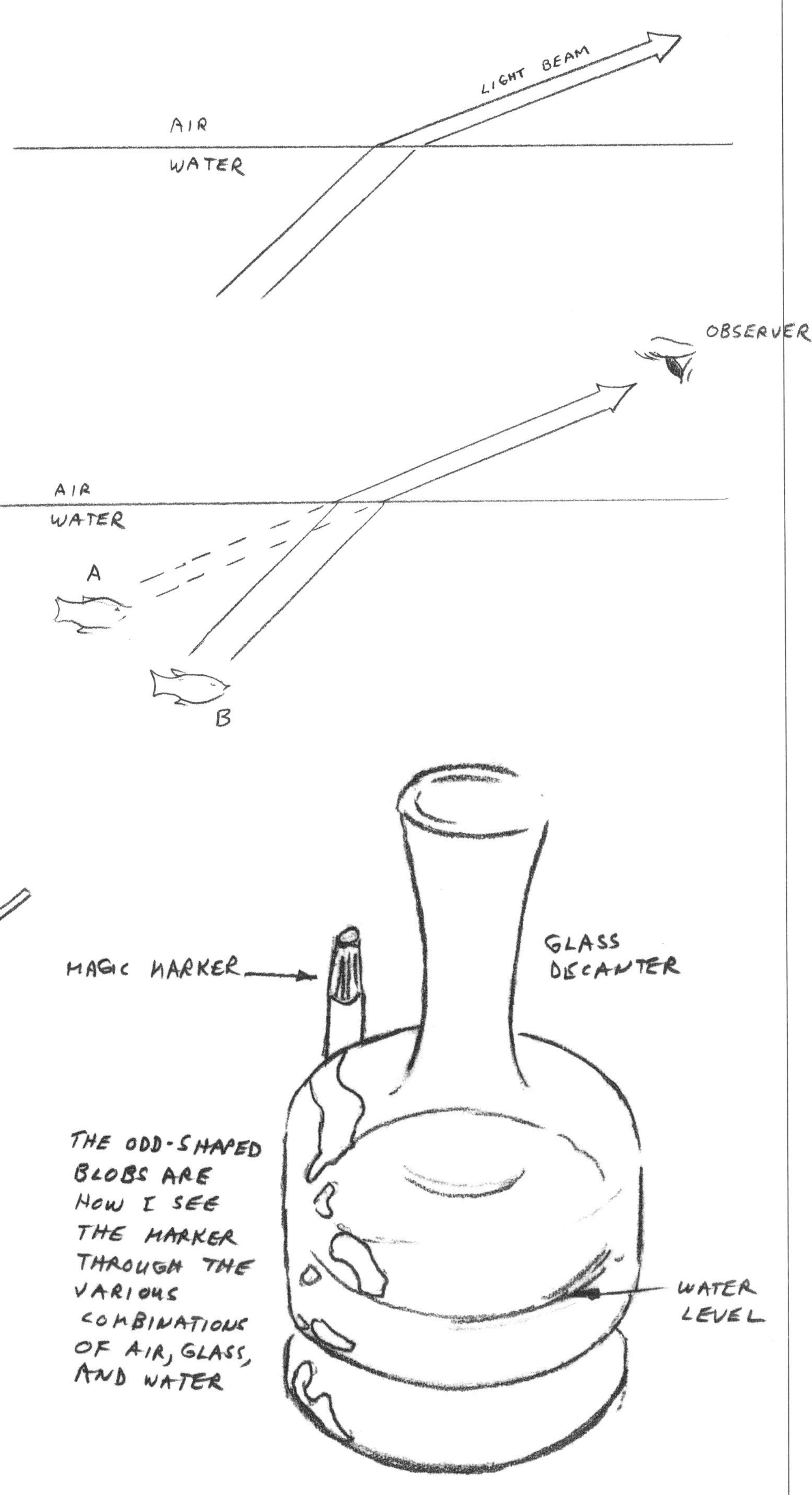

Common Goofs

Certain errors in perspective occur frequently. The following three sketches highlight some of them. See how many you spot and compare your findings to mine. I hope you don't find more than I intended! (Answers are on pages 44 and 45.)

Common Goofs

Common Goofs

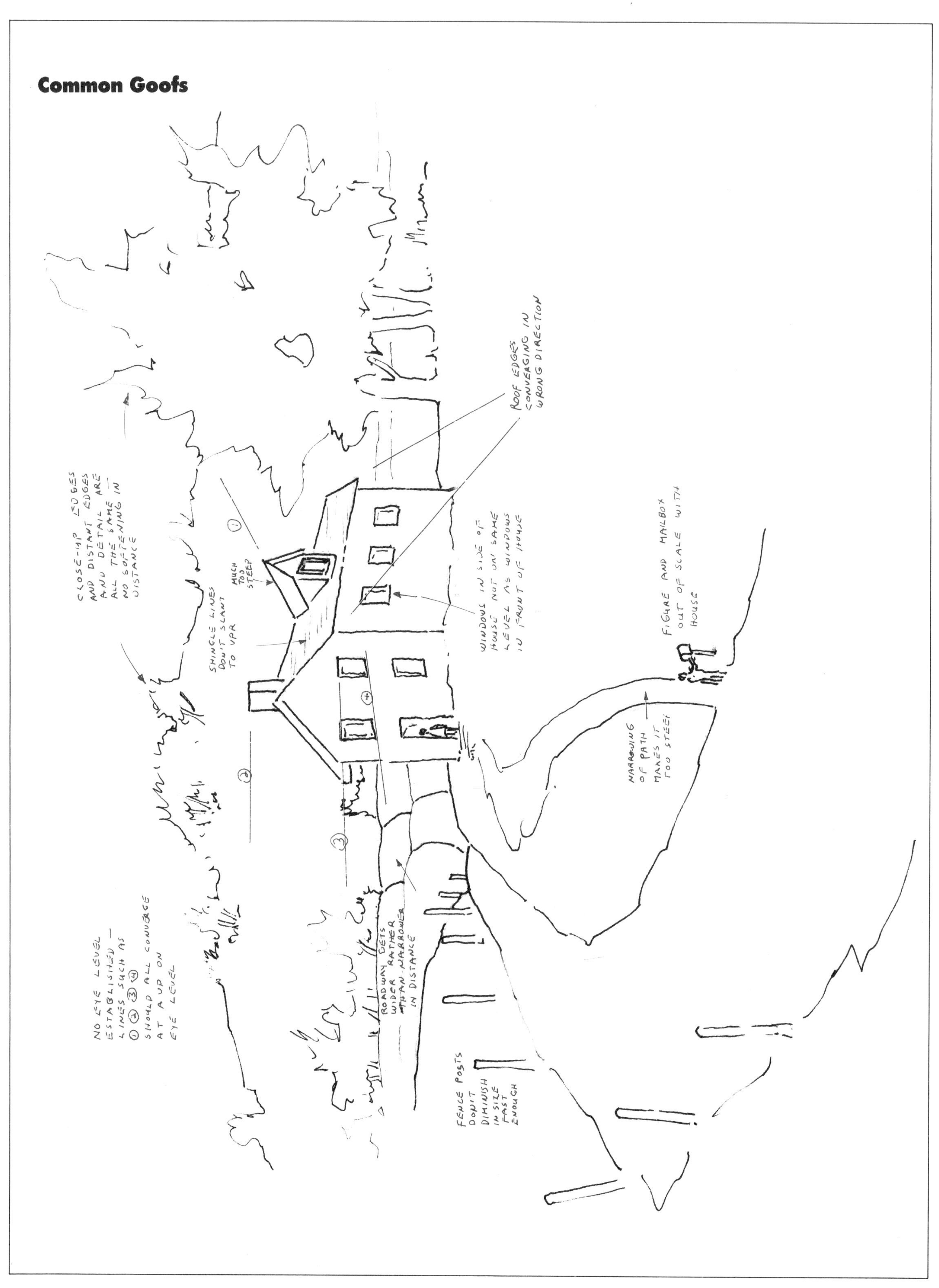

Common Goofs

EYE LEVEL NOT WELL ESTABLISHED — FLAT TOP OF BOTTLE SAYS IT'S HERE.
BUT IF SO, THIS CURVE IS PROBABLY TOO ROUND

SCREW TOP — CHEAP WINE!

THIS GLASS IS SET BACK IN DISTANCE YET IT'S SAME SIZE AS FOREGROUND GLASS

TOP ELLIPSE SHOULD BE NARROWER THAN BOTTOM ELLIPSE

TOP AND BOTTOM EDGES OF LABEL SHOW NO CURVE

SHARP ENDS ON ELLIPSE

SHARP END ON ELLIPSE

REFLECTION MUST LEAN SAME WAY AS TREE

WRONG SHAPE

Limitations

Be a little careful in applying the "rules" of perspective. Although the perspective techniques are powerful tools, they have their limitations. What's "right" mathematically or theoretically may not be "right" for your painting.

Earlier, for example, we discussed an accurate way to space objects, such as poles, in such a way that they would recede properly. Although the method discussed will give you an accurate division of spaces, the result might not always be pleasing.

Several scholars have experimented with this very example by presenting people with pictures of receding poles in which perspective (linear perspective, to be more precise) was used rigidly and asking them to choose between those pictures and ones in which certain liberties were taken. In the latter, the receding poles were not made to bunch together quite as rapidly as perspective "rules" would dictate. People chose strongly in favor of the latter.

It's not that linear perspective is wrong—it pretty much duplicates what a good camera would record—it's just that there's no denying certain psychological urges people have for arranging things in certain ways. In the case of the poles, people seemed not to want them to recede quite as precipitously as they really did. I won't pretend to analyze what makes those things happen—I'm only suggesting that you need to know when a tool has done all it can for you and needs to be abandoned in favor of gut feeling.

Another example: linear perspective is only useful within the normal human "cone of vision"—that is, the area you can see ahead, left and right, up and down, without moving your head or eyes. Beyond that space, in peripheral vision, things get pretty distorted. And beyond that space, linear perspective also gets distorted and ineffective.

A good example of a failing of linear perspective is in painting a very long mural, or perhaps an ornamented frieze along the top edge of a building. It's quite impossible to view such long scenes without actually moving yourself physically and strolling along the length of the picture, or standing so far back that you can see everything at once but can discern little of the picture's detail. What many artists have resorted to in such situations is to break the picture into a series of scenes, each with its own vanishing points, rather than attempt one long scene with a single set of vanishing points.

Despite such limitations, perspective works well for the vast majority of the scenes most of us draw and paint.

Now that you've waded through four workbooks and assimilated everything, let me plead one final time for moderation in the application of what we've covered. Perspective is a tool for helping to gain a sense of depth in a drawing or painting, nothing more. Perspective is not an end in itself. Too rigidly applied, the techniques of perspective could smother an otherwise expressive painting. Don't let them tie you down.